Penguin Education

Understanding Children Talking

Understanding
Children Talking

Nancy Martin, Paul Williams, Joan Wilding,
Susan Hemmings and Peter Medway

Penguin Books

Penguin Books Ltd,
Harmondsworth, Middlesex, England
Penguin Books, 625 Madison Avenue,
New York, New York 10022, U.S.A.
Penguin Books Australia Ltd,
Ringwood, Victoria, Australia
Penguin Books Canada Ltd,
41 Steelcase Road West, Markham, Ontario, Canada
Penguin Books (N.Z.) Ltd,
182–190 Wairau Road, Auckland 10, New Zealand

First published 1976
Reprinted 1976
Copyright © Nancy Martin, Paul Williams, Joan Wilding,
Susan Hemmings, Peter Medway, 1976

The poems 'The Companions' by Yevgeny Yevtushenko, translated
by Robin Milner-Gulland and Peter Levi, S.J.,
translation copyright © Robin Milner-Gulland and Peter Levi, 1962
and 'Girl, Boy, Flower, Bicycle' by M. K. Joseph,
copyright © The University of Auckland, 1954

Made and printed in Great Britain by
Cox & Wyman Ltd, London, Reading and Fakenham
Set in Monotype Plantin

Contents

Preface 7
Introduction 9
1. Reading a Transcript 19
2. Seven Situations 25
3. Inner Worlds 61
4. Work Talk in School 77
5. Roles and Models 144
6. Progress in Talk 168

Preface

This book has grown out of the ongoing work of members of the London Association for the Teaching of English. In 1967 the Association's annual conference was on Talk. As a result of the interest aroused by a week-end's consideration of tape-recordings, a study group was formed to look – in the first instance – at 'discussion', since this term seemed to be used to refer to a great many different occasions and differing kinds of talk.

It was no accident or whim that we began by looking at the talk that went on in small groups of pupils without a teacher. We had come to believe that undirected, informal talk was an important means of learning, but evidence was hard to find. So the obvious starting-point for the group was to collect and transcribe tape-recordings and study them.

As the work developed we found that every talking situation had so many variables that it was very difficult to draw conclusions from it; we found we needed to impose some sort of special focus (or grid) on the talk in its situation to enable us to look *at* it instead of entering in imagination the mini-dramas which all these conversations were. We looked, for instance, at small groups of children discussing a poem (or a story) by themselves or with a teacher participating, and from this drew out some notions about the varying role of a teacher and its effect on the talk. We looked at story-telling, and at argument (as distinct from the kind of discussion which proceeds by additions or expansions of consensus), and we co-operated for several years with John Kerry of the Schools Broadcasting Service who was a member of the group and who was at that time producing his *Speak* programmes.

Between 1967 and 1973 some people dropped out of the group and other people joined it. All in all something like twenty people have contributed to its work. Nor must we forget all the children, parents and teachers whose talk forms the substance of this book, and without whose co-operation our work could not have begun. To them all we are enormously grateful.

The impetus to produce a book was given by the 1971 conference of the National Association for the Teaching of English on *Language Across the Curriculum*, and five of us settled down to it. We have worked on the book as a group and what is here reflects something of all of us and also something of past members of the group, whose transcripts were part of our discussion before this book was thought of.

We want particularly to acknowledge the contribution of Margaret Tucker, whose belief in the educational importance of talk has never wavered, and who was Chairman of the group for four years. Acknowledgement too must be made to Professor James Britton, whose theoretical work on the nature of talk in the educational process has contributed much to our thinking throughout.

The Contributors

PAT D'ARCY
PETER GRIFFITH
RACHEL FARRAR
NELL KEDDIE
HEATHER LYONS
MARGARET FROOD
MARGARET McDONNELL
RAY HEMMING

JOHN KERRY
MARGARET TUCKER
HELEN KING
MARTYN RICHARDS
JENNY DUNN
HENRIETTA DOMBEY
TOM LOWENSTEIN
CHARLES MATTHEWS

The Authors

SUSAN HEMMINGS
NANCY MARTIN
PETER MEDWAY
JOAN WILDING
PAUL WILLIAMS

Introduction

This is a book of talk, and to a less extent a book about talk. Conversation is universally interesting. 'What is the use of a book', said Alice, 'if there are no pictures or conversations', and as we go about our daily lives we all engage in a kind of universal spectatorship as we tell and listen to the hundreds of small tales and anecdotes which form the fabric of the largest part of our conversation. Operations, lost luggage, missed trains, bus stop encounters; quarrels, injustices, griefs, romances; what he said and what she said. We literally tell the stories of our lives – their prospect and their retrospect – as we live them. And, of course, we comment on these happenings, discuss the rights and wrongs, and speculate on generalities, in the process of constructing the realities of our lives in conversation.

Against this background of a universal interest in other people's lives – an inescapable social fact – we offer this collection of tape-recordings of children talking. Most of us are chiefly familiar with children's conversation as it comes to us as adults. We have little opportunity of listening in to their talk to each other. We thought therefore, that parents, and perhaps teachers, would be interested to hear, as it were, children talking to each other, to parents and to teachers.

It may come as a surprise to find how long and how far small groups of children sent off on their own to engage in some directed speech task (such as exploring a poem or rehearsing a talk for a class audience) will often go on their own. They will sometimes talk for forty minutes about one poem or a single incident from a story, or until the tape runs out. Teachers would (probably rightly) be wary themselves of spending so long on a single task, for fear of losing the attention of their pupils, but the children on their own appear to have had no such qualms. The discussion on

9

the poem, 'The Companion' (page 116) is a case in point. But perhaps this is only surprising because adults to a very large extent control the lives of children and within the institutions of school and family probably initiate more talk than the children do whenever the two generations are in social contact. So the patterns of daily living are on the whole determined by us, as are – in general – the patterns of talk that go with them. Outside these patterns of behaviour and talk is the children's 'underground' movement when they are not in contact with adults and where their talk clearly does not closely follow adult norms. Thus teachers (and parents) who are only too aware of children's impatience with the adults' attempts to explain, or instruct, will, we think, be interested to see that children on their own will explore, at length, things that concern them. They are now the initiators, and they are not short of language or ideas. We have known for some time that children can write extremely well; we know relatively little about their capacities for talking. So our primary aim has been to let the children present themselves in their talk with a minimum of comment from us.

Because the spoken language cannot be adequately represented in print, the first section in the book is on 'Reading a Transcript' and we suggest that it would be profitable to read this first. Otherwise, the book is essentially an anthology, though there are problems in making a collection such as this. Real conversations cannot be planned; they happen. And there may or may not be a tape-recorder at hand. So there is a randomness in any such collection – which may not be a bad thing in that this reflects the nature of talk.

Most of us are used to reading what has been *written to be read*; when we read a transcript of *speech* it strikes us as unfamiliar and we are not sure where to put our attention. We may enter the conversation in imagination as if we were actually present – all our attention focused on the meanings being exchanged by the speakers, which, of course, is what we mostly do when we engage in talk ourselves. But we may – as sometimes momentarily in actual conversations – shift our focus of attention to concentrate on the talk itself and become observers rather than listeners. If we do this we perceive some startling things. The actual grammatical structure – for instance – of spoken language in the children's conversations is likely to give us our first shock, and the next one may be to find that adult conversations are very similar in this respect. Then there is the fact that a close focus reveals that many other things than the words uttered are always part of these conversations. Speakers pick up points and make statements or ask questions which, although they are within the terms of the conversation, reflect their individual interests or pre-occupations. This is specially noticeable in the last transcript in the book where we can see how the pattern of individual and social relationships between the speakers is a determining factor in what is said.

The arrangement of the transcripts in sections has been designed to throw light on the way in which talk changes in different situations. There are four sets of loosely grouped conversations. The first group, called 'Seven Situations', are conversations between children on their own or talking to adults in what are essentially non-classroom contexts, although some of them took place in school, and some of the adults happen to be teachers. This section has also a developmental aspect in that it begins with a two-year old talking to his mother, and ends with three very different conversations by twelve-year olds.

The second group, 'Inner Worlds', consists of monologues and dramas and is far away from most adult utterances. Perhaps the nearest we, as adults, get to this kind of talk is in our dreams or day dreams, and of course, in reading literature.

The third, we have called 'Work Talk in School'. Three of the tapes are, in fact, whole lessons and as such provide documentations of conventional learning situations. The third item is of particular interest as it consists of a group of twelve-year-old children teaching themselves as they talk their way through a poem. This parallels the second lesson in this group where a teacher is taking the rest of the class through the same poem.

The last group of conversations, 'Roles and Models', shows older pupils trying out various roles and speaking in the voices that go with them. This, of course, is part of the language learning process anyway and is learnt very early. The 'voices' we use in different situations reflect the different relationships we have with other people present, though these changes of role and voice are not usually, in younger children, consciously adopted. But as older children move nearer to the adult world they consciously try out various roles – see themselves as this kind of person, or that, as they become interested in politics, religion and social matters and foster dreams of what they may become, or the world become.

In the concluding section the question is asked 'is there such a thing as progress in talk?' Can we get better at talking? Clearly there are big differences between the two-year old and the sixteen-year olds. Is this anything to do with school or is it only a matter of growing up and becoming socialized? Can teachers assist the process? These questions were discussed by four members of the team and their discussion recorded and transcribed just as the children's conversations had been. So for anyone interested, in addition to the content of the conversation, there is data here for comparing this open conversation by adults with similar open conversations by the children. Differences there certainly are, but possibly not the expected ones.

One other point needs comment in giving the context of the transcripts. The effect of the tape-recorder on the speakers, varies a great deal. Most often, it is soon forgotten. Once children – or adults – have got used to it the normal social process of listening and talking reasserts itself. From time to time one or other of the speakers may become momentarily aware of it and say 'remember that thing is on', but immediately the magnetic property of talk draws the speakers' attention back into the social focus of the conversation and the recorder is again forgotten.

There are, however, other occasions when the tape-recorder becomes a kind of substitute audience; not the inhibiting, private ear, but an object which is thought of as if it were an audience to whom the speaker addresses his utterance. Some of the monologues which we have referred to as 'Inner Worlds' illustrate this circumstance and, although it is likely that this kind of utterance would go on whether the tape-recorder were there or not, the fact it is does seem to heighten the speaker's sense of an audience. A third kind of response to the recorder is for the speakers to see in it the studio situation, and to modify the conversation in accordance with this sense of a public audience. The twelve-year old boys discussing the two poems illustrate this very clearly.

All the transcripts are unedited and in most cases the introductory note states whether the speakers knew they were being recorded. Where the conversations were too long to be included in full, we have printed a continuous, unedited section and have indicated in the notes how this fitted into its full context.

There are assumptions behind the comments derived from contemporary studies of the spoken language, and these sometimes run counter to popular ideas about speech. For instance people tend to distinguish 'useful' talk from 'mere' talk. People often say '*that* discussion got nowhere', or 'what was that speech all about ? I didn't get much from it', but it does not usually occur to them to make such judgements about most of the talk that goes on most of the time, because their expectations are different. In the case of 'useful' talk there is some kind of transaction afoot; people want information, or want to convince someone else, to argue, explain or inform, and, according to whether their expectations are fulfilled or not, they judge the talk useful or 'pointless'. But it may not be so judged by other participants. Everyone has the choice of speaking or remaining silent, and in this sense all utterances must be purposive for the speaker, though the listener may not find them so. So the distinction would seem to lie more in the circumstances in which the talk arises than in some hard and fast difference between purposive and purposeless talk. The interaction between the members of a group talking together determines whether the conversation is switched on to an 'engage for action' position or to 'relax'; and people learn which situation they are in without its ever being made explicit. Of course, we sometimes make mistakes. If, for instance, in a conversation where people are grumbling or letting off steam one proposes to take action, one can be met by a sudden silence. The unspoken social terms of the conversation have been misinterpreted. The switch has been in the 'relax' position, and the other participants did not really want it switched over to 'engage'. Similarly when one's expectations are for some speech transaction to be fulfilled, and other people have no such expectations, one comes away saying that the talk was pointless, or that no one was serious.

Another feature of speech situations which profoundly affects the kind of talk that goes on is the size of the group. Conversation is talk between two or a few people. If the group gets much larger and attempts to talk together, either some people remain silent, or two or three begin to have a separate conversation. Furthermore, conversation proceeds from the interaction of the various speakers, so its course is socially determined and is therefore very different from the course of a public speech or a class lesson.

Let us look at the difference between talk in large and small groups more closely. The course of conversation, or small group talk, is unpredictable. No one knows at the beginning where it will go or at what point it will end. A person may have something particular to ask or to tell, but beyond this no one knows until it happens. The course of the conversation is mutually determined *as it goes*. What happens in large groups is entirely different. A single person gives a speech, or a lecture or a sermon, but all these are in fact monologues which represent a single speaker's extended and coherent utterance directed to some particular end. It is often predictable what this utterance will be about in general and it is also generally accepted that the listeners will not contribute to the talk until the speaker has finished – or they may not contribute at all.

In school there is, of course, much conversation but most schools are organized in large group units, i.e. classes, and teachers do a good deal of class teaching (or talking). In certain kinds of class lesson the talk is fan-shaped with the teacher at the hub of the fan sending out questions and receiving replies from the other speakers who are scattered along the vanes of the fan as it were. The talk is like this of course because its purpose is to instruct a large group, and it is not essentially different in function from a speech, a lecture, or a sermon. The teacher, like the public speaker, generally has his construct of what the talk is going to be about and by his questions he draws from the children only the responses which will develop his construct, and it is the dynamic of the teacher's initial frame of reference which determines the course of the lesson. Sometimes this sort of lesson gets off course when children initiate their own questions or ideas, but eventually the teacher will say 'Well, now, let's get back to the point' – *his* point in this case, not necessarily the point for all his listeners. This kind of lesson is illustrated by the mathematics and poetry lessons in the section on 'Work Talk'. In contrast the conversation between the six children which we have also included in this section is a real conversation in that no one knows where it will go next because its direction is collectively determined, but the children's unspoken agreement to explore the poem causes them to exclude many things which might come into the conversation were it not constrained in this way by the school situation.

Thus, in work situations, talk is seen as performing some mutual transaction, whether in large groups or small groups and by means of lectures, class teaching or conversation. And it is this situation of an expected talk transaction that people refer to when they say the talk was useful, or pointless, or not serious, etc.

But a great deal of the talk that goes on in our daily lives is not of this kind, and at first sight seems not to have any particular purpose. Consider for instance the phenomenon of the way we sometimes go over a television programme or a film we have liked, and others who have seen it join in a kind of collective re-creation of it. Clearly we are not doing this to inform each other about the play since all parties have seen it. And we have noted earlier the way we exchange the tales of our daily lives. Nothing is too trivial to be recounted if the teller sees it as significant. What is it all in aid of? What is the function of all those apparently purposeless conversations when the social switch is on 'relax'? There are a number of theories and partial theories which can be used to interpret the content and function of such talk; but as yet no theory of sufficient generality has emerged which will fully explain this most ordinary of activities.

We suggest that we all need to work through, sort, organize and evaluate the events of our daily lives. Sleeping, we do this in dreams, waking, in internal monologues and relaxed talk. As individuals we have to assimilate our experiences and build them into our continuing picture of the world; as social beings we need to legitimate the world picture we are continuously constructing and maintaining. So we hold out to others – in talk – our observations, discoveries, reflections, opinions, attitudes and values, and the responses we receive in the course of these conversations profoundly affect both the world picture we are creating and our view of ourselves.

Seen thus, all talk is significant and is the chief means by which we develop as individual and social beings. Furthermore, from this perspective, the difference between what we began by calling purposive talk and apparently random talk is only of importance in that it enables us – in general – to look at the whole conversation of mankind in all its variety and to see it all as an educative process; and – in particular – to understand the function of conversations like ones included here when the four boys are discussing the Beatles, or seven-year-old Terry is talking about her problems at home. And perhaps we should add that an over-emphasis on purposive talk must necessarily militate against relaxed talk and the opportunities this offers for the growth of self-knowledge.

There is a further question that concerned us in making this book. Children spend much of their lives in school, and school has been traditionally concerned with formal education. Should teachers be concerned with a process like conversation which goes on universally anyway ? Viewed developmentally we can say that talk grows as we grow. The question is can we use talk to assist the growing ? To answer this question we need to consider the relation of talk to thinking, to learning (in its school sense) and other school activities such as writing, doing experiments and engaging in practical work of all sorts.

In the earliest stages of language-learning, talk and objects and actions are indivisible. Toddlers name things and ask for things and give orders and make utterances about things they have seen or about people. When they begin to refer to things that happened yesterday or that are not present and part of their immediate surroundings they have made a huge step forward in language learning and in intellectual growth: they have learned to dissociate their speech from the here and now and have begun to be aware of the past and the future. Parents will be familiar with the imagined situations children create by means of language around their playthings. Later they can create imagined situations without the help of playthings and can engage in stories, monologues, dramas and 'poems' where they construct an oral, verbal 'object' arising from their experience and feelings which is organized and sustained by language alone. It is from this kind of spoken utterance that imaginative writing develops and we have illustrated these in the section called 'Inner Worlds'. The significance of these utterances is that they are the chief mode by which young children think.

Parallel to this process (which has been described as the transition from outer speech to inner speech to thought) is the process of developing social communicative speech – speech for others, as distinct from speech for oneself. These two processes may be seen going on side by side in the transcript of the conversation between Stephen and his mother (page 28).

It could be argued that by the time children are seven or eight they have learned to use the basic systems of speech and are also, broadly speaking, literate; and that teachers can therefore concentrate on the more difficult matter of developing children's capacities to use the written language (reading and writing) together with the knowledge that resides in it, leaving talk to look after itself. But a bird's eye look at our schools shows that the situations in which different kinds of talk can happen do not occur universally. We think a school could be, and should be, an environment in which all kinds of talk do – in fact – happen; where children can talk to adults in both formal and informal situations, where purposive, or directed talk goes on – as it always has – and where undirected and unconstrained conversations are also seen as part of the educative process. And here we want to take the argument a stage further, and suggest first, that ordinary talk has an important part to play in the assimilation of new knowledge and new experience; and second, that we need to use our own particular everyday speech to do this.

New knowledge has to be fitted in to existing knowledge, to be translated into terms of one's own experience and re-interpreted, and in this process (which can be called learning) thought and language are very close together. But thought is of great density and speed, and much of it is not within conscious control. If any of it is to be made coherent and communicative a ready-to-hand language is needed to net and give initial shape to the transient flow of ideas, perceptions, images, feelings. One's everyday speech is the nearest-to-hand language that everyone has and is therefore particularly appropriate for new learning situations and first formulations – first drafts of new thinking. And since what has to be sorted out and re-interpreted is not the same for everyone, wide-ranging conversations may well be just what a group of speakers needs. What is regarded as a rambling irrelevancy to one person may be a central sorting out operation to another. But one can only do this sorting out in one's own language, which is the nearest one can come – in the initial stages – to one's own thinking.

Furthermore, any attempt, at this stage, to divert a speaker from *what* he is saying to *how* he is saying it will be a diversion in his thinking. The very features which characterize everyday speech – its looseness, its relative inexplicitness, its focus on the speaker's own vision – themselves give access to thinking. Thus it would seem that everyday speech should be seen as the matrix from which one moves into other modes when they are needed, and to which one reverts in new or difficult situations. This would mean that teachers could not only rest easy with their pupils' everyday language for much more of the time than most of them now think is appropriate, but they could encourage it and create situations where it could occur knowing its importance to a learner.

This, however, is not the whole story. The 'models' of language (spoken and written) that we encounter all the time, without, of course, seeing them as models, are a major influence on our language development. Children's speech approximates to the dominant influences in their lives – their homes, their local community, street, village or school; later it will approximate to other adult models coming from work, peer groups or deliberate approximation to particular speakers. But within schools, or perhaps within education more generally – in text books, and notes, in the specialized terms and conventions of different subjects, and in most teachers' modes of presentation – are the models in which public knowledge is *presented* to children: a very different language, as we have suggested above, from the language in which one explores knowledge for oneself in talk. Most children find it a difficult language to read and more difficult still to write. Their stumbling, inert sentences can be seen in any school note book, but what is often forgotten is that children are not professional historians and scientists but learners, and we would suggest that they are often pushed too hard and too soon towards these imitations of adult transactional language without regard for the needs of the actual situation – which is one of their learning.

In conclusion we would suggest that there are good reasons why every kind of talk should go on in schools and we have therefore included a wide range of talk in this book, but what is crucial in learning is a respect for each child's vernacular, whatever it may be, a respect for everyday speech.

1. Reading a Transcript

1. Pub Talk

A tape made in a bar. Adults talking without knowing they were being recorded.

Woman:	When you make your beer at home is it the same drinking it at home as drinking it at the pub?
1st Man:	No.
Woman:	This is it, isn't it – um sort of –
1st Man:	I've got . . . I've got five gallons on draught right at the moment which I had three pints of last night and I still went up to the pub for a pint of bitter.
Woman:	This is the point. It's not the beer so much. It's sort of . . .
2nd Man:	Frankly if they just served . . .
Woman:	. . . sort of mixture . . .
2nd Man:	coffee or orange squash or lime juice I would still go up the pub. It is a part of life, you know and I think it's a very good part of sound life.
	[*General chat in background*]
Woman:	I'm not sure that coffee would be the same really . . .
1st Man:	No it wouldn't.
Woman:	There's just a sort of slight edge to it that makes you . . .
	[*General chat*]
1st Man:	Why is it because you're going to . . . If I'm honest it is this feeling that everybody knows about – of being lonely and being able to go and socialize with other people . . . drop in . . .

Woman:	and you're not committed in a pub, this is what everyone says to me.
1st Man:	A hundred per cent you're right – Um – you can go up there – I can go up to a pub and my wife says 'Well. Who did you meet' and I can say 'I didn't meet any – anybody' but I have enjoyed myself because I can have a pint, draw it up and I can stand back and I can watch other people and I can enjoy myself. It's ... I think it's loneliness that's ... that's one of the things that's involved there.

Reading a transcript of a conversation like this one (let alone enjoying it) is, for many of us, an acquired skill. Firstly, the page looks messy, and secondly, what we actually read there could with some justification be said to be very boring. The speakers don't seem to have any very clear ideas, or much originality – there doesn't seem to be much point to it all. They are just a group of people passing their time away in a pub, or somewhere similar. But for all this, it is, in its context, obviously, for those people, an effective piece of social exchange. This transcript then, with all its disjointed jerky bits, and its very unriveting subject matter, is chosen to give a fair and square example of what ordinary everyday talk might look like, written down. Also it is given here, in a book which will mainly contain examples of children's talk, in order to remind us what adults' ordinary talk is like, so that we can see how very elliptical, repetitious and (superficially) inconsequential the fully grown person can be – and is, most of the time.

There are many playwrights with a good ear for ordinary talk, but they are usually also skilled in giving it an impact which, in real life, it does not actually have, while at the same time maintaining a fine illusion of reality. But since transcripts are talk, not dialogue in a play, the skills one needs to read, interpret and enjoy them are not necessarily the same ones which we take along to the theatre or use to read a play inside our heads. Nor does the transcript reader have the advantage of hearing full-bodied voices, unless the tape is to hand.

The transcriber has to try to be as true as possible to the original. Since any tape is likely to contain much which is barely audible (especially when subjects do not know that they are being recorded), and much that is simultaneously uttered, this is always a difficult task. Perhaps those who are interested to learn how to read transcripts most effectively will already have had the helpful initial experience of making one.

It is, of course, virtually impossible to transcribe, or notate, everything that is being transmitted by the speakers. Even where there is only one person speaking, and speaking clearly, there is always the problem of how to convey the actual emphasis, the implied gestures and significant faltering or pausing. Voice quality, and facial expressions can, for example, give an additional layer of meaning to the actual words spoken, to the extent that they may even show that the speaker means quite the opposite of what he is actually transcribed as saying! And, of course, the difficulties of accurately notating a conversation where *several* people are taking part, interrupting, speaking simultaneously, gesturing, muttering, hesitating and laughing, are many times greater.

At the moment there are no fixed rules for transcribers to follow. Most try, by putting down the spoken words, and near-words, in exactly the order they are spoken, to achieve at least a limited accuracy. Pauses, if significant, are often marked, and also laughter. Perhaps one day a complex notation will become standard, whereby all the other gestures which are adjuncts to speech, and all inflections within speech, can be simultaneously 'orchestrated', in much the same way as musicians like Stockhausen have experimented. Meanwhile, an accurate transcript where what is actually said is carefully written can still be extremely useful and revealing, even when used completely without the original sound recording.

2. Adult Students' Discussion

A group of adult students explaining to another group about a film they are planning to make. They know they are being recorded and this is one of a whole series of recorded discussions made by themselves for analysis of their course.

M: I see. What's the film going to be about?

C: [*Laughter.*] We haven't exactly decided, have we?

Pat: No, we've um thought about one or two um meditations to the possibilities – we thought perhaps it was – this was Debbie's idea actually – that it wasn't a very good idea to attempt people speaking because the er problems of synchronizing sound and speech is probably er you know er lips to sound is probably beyond us . . . and, er I wasn't very keen on the idea of doing er a sort of acting type film in which we made up a story and then acted it out. We . . . we thought perhaps we were attracted to the idea of a documentary (Group: Mm.) of some kind and er was it you . . . you were suggesting er . . . not people . . .

C: Well there was a social comment of some sort, traffic versus countrysides, that kind of combination . . .

June: Oh, that's what we're doing.

[*Much overtalk*]

We've got some ideas [*?*] you can use if you like . . .

June: . . . country districts play the same games as children do in urban districts.

C: Well really all we were talking about was doing some sort of social commentary but the actual content I think is very undecided . . .

June: Well it's not original anyway . . . [*laughter*]

C: Do we care?

Group: I don't think so.

Reading a transcript where we do not have access to the original tape means bearing in mind the main differences between the written and the spoken word. Speech is very much a process, and will show evidence of many changes in mid-stream, of censoring, of re-starting. Talk between people in a group will show a certain jumping about from point to point, 'irrelevant' interruptions, and speakers continuing with *their* idea despite what has been previously said on a different topic by an interim speaker. The transcriber may often have difficulty tracing the sequence of the conversation, which may well be, in some cases, because there simply *isn't* any sequence. Talk is not usually sequential in the way that a written piece is – and it is best to remember that transcripts, being 'written talk' rather than actual prose, or composed dramatic dialogue, are bound to be full of just those kinds of inconsequence and confusion, pauses and contradictions which the composer of the *written* word would normally completely iron out.

If we took Pat's speech from the second extract and asked her to make a written account of it, maintaining all the basic ideas, we might get something like this:

> When we were considering the possibilities, Debbie suggested that perhaps we should not try to film people speaking, because the problems of synchronizing lips to sound was probably too hard for us. I was not very keen, either, on making the kind of film that involved acting out a story we had made up. On the whole, we were attracted to the idea of some kind of documentary . . .

Pat would feel that her speech, taken from the context of the discussion, would need a more careful structure. She might need to mention details in the *written* form ('film', 'on the whole'), which in the context of the conversation could be carried implicitly (because they all knew about the filming and had shared common problems with it). The written form would also expel the little fillers like 'er' and 'um' because their important functions in speech – giving extra thought time, assessing your listeners' reactions and so on – are not relevant to the writer, who can allow himself the act of reflection and censorship without interrupting the flow of the finished version.

More complex is the way in which the written form would show a change in syntax. It would doubtless conform to formal sentence patterns with a deliberate use of balanced clauses – as we feel are relevant to literacy. Heard on the tape in talk form, Pat's meaning is perfectly clear. No one would feel that she was speaking incorrectly in grammatical terms, or that what she was saying did not make sense. In the social context of conversation, the speaker can easily risk a weakening of syntax, especially where an experience which has been shared by the talkers is being discussed. ('. . . the er problems of synchronizing sound and speech is probably you know er lips to sound . . .') But to express the same ideas outside the context of talk in process, Pat would need a firmer grammatical structure to ensure her meaning was conveyed – to people who had not necessarily shared the filming experience with her.

Reading a transcript, therefore, means witholding the kind of expectations one usually has of the written word. We may well find certain grammatical structures in transcripts which in any other written form might seem inappropriate. It is true to say, however, that in all but very extreme cases the grammar of the spoken word is fundamentally the same as the literate grammar. There is, for instance, no *basic* difference in word order. The literate form both tightens and elaborates upon the speech form, but they do not use different grammars in any real linguistic sense.

If a piece of talk, in transcript form, seems disjointed, repetitious, or illogically structured, it will, of course, still be weighted with meaning. We can usually deduce reasons for the various shifts in structure when we analyse the transcript as a whole, later on. Talk is such a very different process from writing that we cannot always expect to find the same kinds of language within it. For these reasons, reading transcripts needs a fairly specialized kind of attention, and the kind of imaginative effort which can project the reader into the aural and social context of the talkers.

2. Seven Situations

Children with and without adults, in non-classroom contexts

We begin by presenting seven conversations which illustrate many of the points about talk made in the introduction. We have called this group of transcripts 'Seven Situations' to emphasize the fact that a conversation is part of behaviour and always arises from some situation of doing, or feeling or thinking. Here are children talking to each other, or to adults, in what are essentially non-classroom contexts, although some of them took place in school and some of the adults happen to be teachers.

The age of the children varies from Stephen, who is two years and ten months, to the schoolboys in the last three transcripts who are twelve.

We have argued in the introduction that all talk is functional and in introducing each of the seven conversations we have tried to suggest what these functions are, and to relate the talk to the children's stage of development. For instance, Stephen (tape 1) at two years and ten months is at the stage of language learning where his play needs to be sustained by talk. He needs to say what he is doing in order to do it. He doesn't really need his mother's replies and questions: it has been observed that children at this stage of their language development need a *sense of a listener*, though in the talk that accompanies their imaginative play they, like Stephen, don't want the interruption that real conversation would be.

Again, in tape 3, Terry and Anne, aged seven, are engaged with a mathematical puzzle, and this kind of 'doing' offers the opportunity for sharing experiences – things that are causes of anxiety (from Terry), things that are causes of pleasure (Anne) and plans of consolation (Anne). In sharing these kinds of confidences Terry and Anne are doing what every adult does, but the situation illustrates the point that it is often easier to engage in intimate conversation when you are doing something else which does not make too great demands on your attention (compare the talk that goes on in a launderette, or on an allotment).

'A Mealtime Conversation' (tape 2) between the six- and five-year olds illustrates the stage children go through when they have mastered language enough to demonstrate their control by playing with it. Puns, ('corn off the cob'), verbal jokes, tricks involving understanding the rules of the game with words ('Uncle Dick'), rhymes and riddles all play a large part in children's talk at this stage.

'Rule-making' (tape 4) is very different from those that precede and follow it. In the first place fifteen people are talking together, thirteen nine-year-old children, one of their mothers and their teacher, and here the large size of the group profoundly affects the kind of talk that goes on (see Introduction pp. 9–18). For all members of a group of this size to contribute to a conversation there is necessarily a common purpose which everyone understands and works towards even if they cannot keep it in mind all the time. In this case they were all trying to decide the 'rules' for sleeping, getting up and having breakfast; i.e. it arose from their common need to decide things and to act upon them, so its subject matter is, in general, predictable and, generally, 'to the point'. Furthermore, in the way it proceeds it is different from the other conversations which move along as the result of the interaction of what the various speakers say to each other – which is, of course, how all conversations proceed. This one, however, is also governed in a way that the others were not by the general acceptance that there are decisions to be made. It is performing a mutual transaction, and in this sense could be called a 'useful' conversation, whereas, at first sight, none of the other conversations in this group of seven are of this kind – with the possible exception of tape 5 ('The Aryans'). What we have in mind in selecting these seven conversations is to try to show that all the conversations are useful in the educative sense that all have a function for the speakers. We think, as we read the transcripts, the speakers can be seen to be assimilating their experiences, coming to terms with all sorts of things and demonstrating an increasing mastery of language for different social and individual purposes.

The last three conversations ('The Aryans', 'The Beatles' and 'Garbling Words') are between a group of boys from the same group (twelve-year olds) in the same school. They are accustomed to talking together and to their teacher, and they are accustomed to using the tape-recorder a great deal by themselves for all sorts of purposes. They like to record their conversations and to listen to them and re-engage in the topics discussed. These three transcripts are fully commented upon by their teacher.

Finally, we should like to comment on the relationships between the children and the adults in those conversations where an adult is present (Nos. 1, Stephen and his mother; 3, Terry, Anne and Mrs Berkeley; and 4, children, teacher and a parent.) In these conversations the adults have a clear view of their role as *adults* in a conversation between children and themselves. They do not participate as equals, as they might were they talking to other adults. On the one hand, Stephen's mother keeps herself very much in the background as the kind of listener or availability person that she thinks Stephen wants as 'background' to his play. Mrs Berkeley, the student-teacher in the Primary School, operates a similar role; she is there if they want to talk to her.

On the other hand, in tape 4, 'Rule-making', the two adults, the children's teacher and the mother of one of them play a kindly but directive role – 'joint Chairmen' at least – in helping the children to arrive at decisions, and not hesitating to push the adult view that some rules need to be arrived at. How tactfully they allow the final decision to be reached that it is time for bed!

And, of course, this conversation shows that one can participate in a conversation for its own sake, but can also, from time to time, shift focus on to what is happening – where the conversation is going and how the other talkers are behaving, i.e. we can be simultaneously aware both of the conversation and the speakers and their needs. This is probably a mature capacity. Where a need is directly expressed, as Terry expresses her mother's money problems, very young children can shift their focus from their own expressive utterances to utterances that take account of the other speakers and their needs. But, of course, such needs are more often expressed indirectly – in terms of whatever is being talked about – and here such awareness is rare among children. This issue is raised in the conversation between the four adults in the last section of this book (Progress in Talk). It suggests, perhaps, that a very valuable role for adults in children's conversations is a background facilitating one.

1. Early Language Learning: Stephen and his mother

Stephen, two years and ten months, is playing with his trains while his mother is busy nearby. She takes the role of an unobtrusive but interested listener. Her voice is very quiet and makes almost no demands for a reply from Stephen. He, on his part, does not want to engage in a conversation but he does want a listener who keeps gently assuring him that she is listening, which is just what his mother, on the whole, does. So, in fact, this exchange of talk is not a conversation. All parents will be familiar with the way children at this age accompany their play by saying what they are doing as they do it and planning aloud what may happen next, with occasional references to things that happened yesterday or in the recent past.

The function of this kind of monologue for a child is to enable him to create and sustain his imaginary situations. It is thought that without words his play would be merely manipulative – pushing things here and there; and it is the flow of language as he plays which enables him to transform the toys into situations which include his own past experiences.

In such an activity a real two-way conversation can be seen to be an interruption – as when his mother corrects his word 'cobway' – more to herself than to him perhaps – and says, 'Oh you mean cobwebs!' and Stephen says, 'You can read that book for a minute . . . while I play with my trains'. Then he goes back into the talk which surrounds and sustains his imaginary situation of trains, signal boxes and engine drivers.

However, later in the conversation, after his mother says 'I must do a bit of work', he shifts his focus and tries to draw her into his activity. At this point the talk becomes a real conversation, no longer talk accompanying play but concerned with things that have happened and which they both know about.

Stephen:	That's going on . . . on . . . on the carriages. That's going to go next to the carriages – You see? And we shall put on the brake, you see? We shall put on the brake. We got the diesel trains haven't we? I play with that, then Jonathon played with that train and then I played with those two trains. And he played with Punch and Judy when Daddy was ready to go to work.
Mother:	Did he?
Stephen:	Yes, he did . . . . . . Then he fell down like that . . . Oh that's going to go – on this do you see? And then it's got a (. . . ? . . .) like that. Mine's a black engine isn't it? And that engine is going to be on that train you see. And if you do have a truck in there it won't work.
Mother:	Won't it?
Stephen:	No.
Mother:	Why not?
Stephen:	'Cos it won't. – There's two engines, there's lots of trains. I want my socks off – the fire will warm them won't it? Yes. My nose was a bit runny so I wiped it on that.
Mother:	Did you?
Stephen:	That will warm it up – there – I've put them my socks on the fire-guard so the fire will warm them up you see. Oh – look! you see? The book shouldn't be under there should it? No! No! I stepped over that train. Then he will go under that bridge too. Do you like this bridges? Bridges are cobway isn't it? And when in't they? I know – cobway go . . . go . . . that's cobway falling down?
Mother:	Is it?
Stephen:	Yes it is – you see – and when the train is covered in cobway the man said it's so stiff isn't he? – The trains are covered with cobway when the man says 'Oh, I'm so stiff!'
Mother:	Oh you mean cobwebs!

Stephen:	And why didn't he ? You can read that book for a minute.
Mother:	Can I ? thank you.
Stephen:	Yes, while I play with my trains. That's the signal and the signal box is under the radiogram. An when ... at the moment really ... It's got ... diesel train. Must have one on the diesel train mustn't we ? That will drive it off anyway. That man will drive it off on the roof – that man is on the roof driving it – you see ? And why don't they lie down for ? He's got a stick and why hasn't he got a stick for ?
Mother:	To bonk people with.
Stephen:	Why ? ... Oh people get upset. And he-he-don't bonk – I take the stick away from him and (... ? ...) bonk me.
Mother:	Will you ?
Stephen:	Yes, I'll put him in the water.
Stephen:	I'll put him down at the bottom and – kkk – pop up ! Ha – wouldn't that be interesting ? Mm – and like – I spit water out and the water say yes I will stay there and I will spit it out. I'll get on the biggest one and dive in the swimming bath and pop up again ! Daddy always pops in the swimming bath already. Yes ! and he pops in his head down – Yes he does. – Yes and then I gobbled – and Daddy pulled me out of the water didn't he ?
	The fire will warm the train ups – the trains up won't it ? And did you do – now two engines – on that – one – it won't work – you see ? And it – and I drawed on that one on there – Yes I did – I like drawing on trains – Do you ? Yes I do.
Mother:	I must do a bit of work – if you want to go and play with your trains for a bit hey ?
Stephen:	I don't want to – it's just setting off – well I can't – it's just setting off and I can't catch it – it's just setting off now.
Mother:	Where is it going ?

Stephen:	That way – and that one is going that way and he's got a train and a little engine going that way and it's got a truck hasn't it ? – Do you know what does go on trucks ?
Mother:	Oh, all sorts of things – coal, animals, sometimes – cows . . .
Stephen:	I put – the fly didn't go down the drain this morning did it ?
Mother:	The spider ?
Stephen:	No. We didn't tell about that did we ? No – it was trying to slip down – it was trying to go down wasn't it ? Yes !
Mother:	What did it do ?
Stephen:	Oh, if the spider came up it would bite me wouldn't it ?
Mother:	It might.
Stephen:	And why don't it ? Why *will* it ?
Mother:	It might be frightened.
Stephen:	Why ?
Mother:	You're so much bigger than a tiny spider, aren't you.
Stephen:	Tiny, tiny little spiders like Susan aren't they ? Yes – and I got a windscreen [?] on my stick aren't [?] I ? and when I bring it, it won't go will it ? . . . [*After cutting the next few minutes . . .*]
Stephen:	Oh look – you broken that train ! You mend it for me ! – I will mend it –
Mother:	Mm, you're the train mender.
Stephen:	The soldier didn't fall off did he ?
Mother:	No, he didn't.
Stephen:	No – he . . . didn't he ? that one didn't fall off didn't he ? Shall I put it together again ? There – I got up on my lap – your lap myself didn't I ? You didn't pick me up did you ?
Mother:	No – you're a big boy now.
Stephen:	I put my feet down there – so that they won't get get out of the way will it ? When I was a little thin boy I used to [build] ? myself – like Daddy – Mm – I did –

31

Mother:	You used to what ?
Stephen:	A little boy – I used to be a little boy years ago weren't I ?
Mother:	Mm, was it a very long time ago ?
Stephen:	Yes it was – it was –
Mother:	How long ?
Stephen:	At six o'clock I was a tiny boy like Daddy aren't I ? And when I'm a big boy like Daddy I always put that fire on – and know how to put it off. Do you ?
Mother:	It burns and burns until there isn't anything left . . .
Stephen:	I see.

2. Mealtime Conversation: Katy, Lucy and Lisa

The children here are five-, six- and six-and-a-half-years old. Katy and Lucy, sisters, were visiting Lisa, and having lunch at her house. They are school friends. No adult was present while they were talking, nor were they aware of the tape recorder.

In their conversation, narrative at first seems to be the style into which they settle, the two sisters as cooperating raconteurs, and Lisa as the listener. The first idea springs from the food itself, and soon, through a series of ingenious associative links, the sisters embark on their tales of recent amusing happenings. The light-hearted mood is continued with a game of punning in which all three take an equal part, and then there is another game, this time 'feet-under-the-table' played out in 'baby' voices. Again every one takes turns, and rules seem to be evolved.

These children enjoy their mealtime against the social fabric of their conversation – and show they know all sorts of knacks of co-operation needed for this kind of talk. Tellers and listeners take it in turns, other speaker's ideas are taken up, one's own ideas politely (if temporarily) discarded . . . just some of the ways in which they show they know how to behave to produce an amicable mealtime conversation. Mealtimes seem almost ideal for such friendly encounters.

Lucy: . . . delicious dinners.

Lisa:	We have delicious dinners . . . we don't get much of it, though.
Lucy:	We have corn OFF the cob at school, don't we? [*Pause – then more quietly*] We have corn off the cob.
Lisa:	Mmm.
Katy:	Shall I tell you something? I . . . once I pretended . . . I took a drink of water and then . . . 'Daddy, my tooth's come out' . . . 'n he said, 'Ooo, goodness gracious, eat up and put it in your mouth again.' He didn't know really what . . . so I picked it up . . . my tooth was still there but I'd eaten it up.
Lucy:	But it's really corn.
Lisa:	Mmm.
Katy:	Yes, but it looks so like teeth.
Lucy:	Once Daddy was very naughty. He . . . he played a trick on us when he was on the phone, didn't he?
Katy:	Mmmm.
Lucy:	That he was a puppet show man.
Katy:	Yes, he was called Mr Dick.
Lucy:	Yes, and I said he wanted just a . . . and you said, 'It's Mr Dick on the phone!' didn't you?
Katy:	Yes, 'n I went running to the phone.
Lucy:	And he played a big trick on me, didn't he?
Lisa:	Who was on the phone?
Katy:	It was really Daddy but he pretended to be called Uncle Dick.
Lucy:	Look, Lisa, what's your [?] name?
Lisa:	Your uncle?
Katy:	No, not my uncle – really Daddy, but he played a trick.
Lisa:	No, but what . . . but was he pretending to be your uncle?
Katy:	Yes.
Lucy:	No.
Katy:	Yes, he was.
Lucy:	What's your name? [*Jumbled on the tape, something about mothers and fathers*] . . . and things like

	that. Is this your [*?*]
Katy:	Are you jewish?
Lisa:	I want to play . . . yes . . . I would say, 'My name's Rosemary'. You know.
Katy:	And that's why I keep [*?*] so you mustn't copy her name.
Lisa:	Rosemary? [*Pause*] Not M'ree.
Lucy:	Rose-mair-ee.
Lisa:	I said R . . . Rose-MAIR-ee.
Lucy:	Rose Mair EE? You mustn't copy our Mummy's name either.
	[*Pause.*]
Lisa:	Rose DAIR ee.
Lucy:	Oh. Rose DAIR ee.
Lisa:	From the dairy, you know, when you get the milk from.
Lucy:	Yes.
	[*Pause.*]
Katy:	Is this somebody's foot? Is this little Lucy's foot?
Lucy:	Yeh.
Katy:	Is this little Lisa's foot?
Lisa:	No [*laughs*].
Lucy:	Tis!
Katy:	Is this little Lucy's foot?
Lucy:	Yes.
Lisa:	Is this little Lucy's foot?
Lucy:	Yes.
Katy:	No.
Lucy:	No.
Lisa:	Yes it is.
Katy:	Stop moving. [*Pause.*] Somebody do it to me.
Lucy:	Is this . . . Lisa's foot?
Katy:	No [*giggles*].
Lucy:	Now, Katy . . .
	[*Pudding brought in by Lisa's mother.*]
Lisa:	Yummy mousse.
Katy:	Pink! Ymmm.
Lisa:	'stead of chocolate.

Katy:	Scrumptious.
Lucy:	Scrumptious.
Katy:	. . . me. That's my dish.
Lucy:	That's my dish . . . that's your dish, Katy.
Adult:	I'm putting on the radio to listen to the news.
Lisa:	News ? Yuk.

3. While Engaged in a Mathematical Puzzle: Terry, Anne and an adult

This conversation takes place in a primary school classroom between two girls of seven, Terry and Anne, and a married woman training to teach. In this class small groups of children engage, simultaneously, in different activities which they can choose and which they change frequently during the school day. The age range in the class is from five to seven and for much of the time children of different ages work together as they might in a family. The children are natural and friendly with each other and with their teachers, and a quiet buzz of conversation accompanies their work.

Terry and Anne are engaged with a mathematical puzzle and Mrs Berkeley is sitting at their table listening and observing, unobtrusively, like Stephen's mother. The conversation that follows shows the need that Terry has to talk out her troubles not only because she needs sympathy but because she needs to understand her own situation. Mrs Berkeley and Anne, also, gain something from their participation, perhaps.

Terry:	Mummy's really fed up, she doesn't know what to do and so she just . . . she just gets up the wall and shouts that's all she can do . . . laugh [*laughs*] . . .
Mrs Berkeley:	Umm . . . does she get
Terry:	. . . she gets upset sometimes and she cries and then she gets all . . . and she wipes her eyes and she gets all upset again, proper old pip but when it first happened I used to cry . . . when I was in bed I used to . . . I used to cry my eyes out until I was soaking wet.

Anne:	I'll just have to put that in the corner
Mrs Berkeley:	Umm . . .
Terry:	Umm . . . Mummy's so unhappy, I feel sorry for her
Anne:	. . . seven
Terry:	I think that teacher is very nice, she's very nice to me
Anne:	What was?
Terry:	You know that . . . teacher there
Anne:	Who, Miss Brown?
Terry:	. . . er . . .
Anne:	. . . she's nice
Terry:	but Mummy, Mummy . . .
Anne:	[*Inaudible.*]
Terry:	She can't do nothing without it though . . . I'm fed up as well, I sleep walk.
Mrs Berkeley:	What?
Terry:	I sleep-walk because of Daddy, I don't know why I just sleep-walk and think he's there and I just sleep-walk, and I touch the wall and I think . . . ah! [*Noises of agreement*] . . . and I get all frightened.
Anne:	I'm frightened in the dark.
Terry:	I used to go to bed with the light off, but now I can't. I think of monsters coming near Daddy and eating him and killing him . . . ooh . . . when I've got the light on [*Assenting noises from Mrs Berkeley and Anne*] . . . I'm frightened for him, then it frightens me, . . . my Daddy's not around, because I keep getting up and crying, . . . often I'm frightened when Daddy's not here.
Mrs Berkeley:	. . . One, two three . . .
Anne:	[*Inaudible.*]
Anne:	So do I, I scream.
Terry:	He was . . . he was very fond of me . . . I was . . . he used to call Doris . . . his either nuisance or baby, she used to cry too much. He called me cherub.
Anne:	Yes.
Terry:	My Mum . . . she isn't well

36

Anne:	Mrs Berkeley, on Sunday I've got to go to a party.
Terry:	Do you know how to spell it.
Anne:	I do, G-A-N-RGRNA
Terry:	Grana.
Anne:	G . . . that's [*inaudible*] HAKN umm . . . Marco.
Terry:	Funny name isn't it.
Anne:	I know, because it's . . . umm . . . Italian. Mrs Berkeley, Mummy bought . . . Mummy bought me Mummy bought me some new clothes once, she bought me a new pair of shoes and when we went in the shop she asked for a [*inaudible*] they were white . . . twenty-two square holes right up to the [*inaudible*] . . . they've got pink bows . . . with a zip up . . .
Terry [*Simultaneously*.]:	My Mummy, my Mummy can't . . .
Anne:	and I've got a pair of gloves and I've got a dress with white lace round the collar, and I've got a . . .
Terry:	She can't [*inaudible*] . . . we have to shake out our money-box, she's got a jar full of money but she hasn't got much.
Anne:	Mrs Berkeley, are you going to record any minute of what we've been saying.
Mrs Berkeley:	Yes, honey.
Terry:	Do you mean . . . [*inaudible*] . . . I've got about ten coins in my money box, I've got . . . [*inaudible*] . . . in my money box, and Mummy's got her own money box, and Mummy's got to count them as well.
Mrs Berkeley:	Is that all you've got ?
Terry:	Yes, Mummy's got some money in her purse but not much, she can't hardly pay the bills.
Anne:	Do you know what I'll do Terry:
Terry:	. . . about sweet shop down the road.
Anne:	Terry . . . [*inaudible*] . . . [*general murmur*] . . . Terry I can put all my threepenny bits in little envelopes, then I can stick the tops down and I can post them through your door.

Terry:	That's what she does, one day she posted . . . she posted a letter to me, I thought it was a letter, I opened it there was a bit of clay . . . I opened the clay out and there was a sixpence inside the clay she done it . . .
Anne:	It was from my money box.
Mrs Berkeley:	You're very rich aren't you? Who gives you all that money.
Anne:	I save up threepenny bits and sixpences and pennies and halfpennies.
Terry:	So do I, I save up pennies and halfpennies and threepenny bits.

4. Rule-making: fourteen nine-year olds and two adults

This discussion was part of a meeting of fourteen nine-year olds, their teacher, the mother of one of them and two student teachers (who do not speak in this section of the transcript). The party was away from home on a school field week. The girls were to sleep in a cottage and the boys in tents. The meeting was held after supper on the first evening of the week to decide on what domestic arrangements needed to be made.

A general eagerness to help in taking decisions about getting-up times, or taking on tasks is apparent – toast making, for instance, or morning inspection of sleeping quarters. The children seem to accept that a situation in which they are consulted is a fair one, and consequently, fall in with suggestions that seem fair – rather than extreme or provocative such as Peter's suggestion of getting up at half past eleven. Clearly, they like to be consulted and their eagerness to volunteer suggests a situation which is moving towards one where, if invited, the children could arrange their own affairs.

The discussion of who is going to wake the children in the morning starts as a sub-conversation, dominates the general discussion for a time, then goes back underground. The subject reappears later at the end of this section of the transcript.

The discussion has clear undertones of sexual awareness both here and later. Beverly comments, 'They're not going to come up to our bedroom!' and later expresses alarm at boys coming in when the girls 'are in awkward positions'! At this point none of the adults present mediate the discussion though the teacher is appealed to when the subject comes up again later. Karen says, 'Mrs Lyons have you told everybody about girls not going in the boys' tents and . . .' It is interesting that it is the girls who are pre-occupied with the subject; the boys' lack of interest is indicated by Alan starting a different conversation with Mrs West about the earwigs in his tent. The teacher brings the two conversations together.

The discussion ends with the teacher asking questions which expect a single answer: 'Have we made that rule? Are there any more rules we need to make?' and with the children's request to go to bed. The unusualness of the request is explained by the fact that the first night away from home in bunks, tents or sleeping bags – and with other children – had been eagerly looked forward to.

One needs also to say that, for the adults, it's not altogether spontaneous talk; they are consciously setting out here to give the children experience in the kind of talk which leads to decision by common sense reflection and majority agreement. But for the children the discussion is a 'natural' one and has no conscious undertones. We could say that the adults have to find a balance between the twin functions of the conversation – on the one hand to get the rules made, and on the other to give practice in the art of making them. Adults, and especially teachers, are often in this situation with children. Perhaps it is relatively rare to have a conversation between grown ups and children where both sides enjoy equal spontaneity?

Teacher:	What did we decide about the breakfast bell, I couldn't hear your suggestions.
Nicholas:	Breakfast bell goes about 9 o'clock –
Mrs West:	Ugh.
Nicholas:	And when we wake up, until 9 o'clock, we can play in the bracken field.
Teacher:	I think that's too late for breakfast.
Mrs W:	Yes.
Teacher:	I think 8 o'clock breakfast.

39

Children:	7 oclock
	8 o'clock
	8 o'clock
	7

Teacher: 8 o'clock I think we ought to say.

Nicholas: 8 o'clock for breakfast –

Teacher: Yes, you'll be awake much earlier. You'll be ready for breakfast by then.

Nicholas: – and then you can get dressed and go straight into the bracken field.

Beverly: [*Writing it down*] Eight o'clock breakfast bell.

Peter: Half past eleven.

Teacher: All right, eight o'clock breakfast bell, eight? What's the latest time people ought to get up, do you think?

Peter: Half past eleven.

Teacher: . . . as long as you're in time for breakfast.

Michael: A quarter past eight.

Teacher: You'll miss your breakfast then, won't you.

Beverly: [*In middle of argument with boys*] Oh no you're not waking *us* up.

Rachel: Oh yes they are.

Girls: I'm waking . . . I'll wake you up.

Beverly: They're not going to come in our bedroom!

Marie: No, I'll wake you up.

Anthony: The first one to wake up, wakes the others up.

Alan: Yes.

Mrs W: Can we have a time before which nobody is to make a sound?

Everybody: Yes.

Mrs W: Please? . . .

Teacher: No, in the morning.

Mrs W: In the morning, if you wake up before . . .

Rachel: Seven o'clock.

Mrs W: . . . Quarter past, yes, seven o'clock.

Teacher: If you wake up before 7 o'clock . . .

Mrs W: You just read books and keep quiet.

—:   Probably, how do we know what time it is? Can we go in the bracken field?

Teacher:	Most people have got um –
Wendy:	. . . in the bracken field ?
Teacher:	Has any girl got a watch ?
Karen:	Me.
—:	Karen.
Teacher:	So there'll be a watch in the girls' bedroom.
Marie:	Could she put it where everybody can see it ?
Mrs W:	I've got an alarm clock upstairs and it will go off at about twenty past seven.
Girls:	Oh.
Mrs W:	And it makes a noise to wake the devil. Let alone half a dozen girls.
Teacher:	Have both boys in their tents, I mean both lots of boys got watches ?
Peter:	Yeah – me.
Michael:	No.
Anthony:	Where . . . ?
Teacher:	Michael's got one. Peter, are you in the same tent as Michael ?
Peter:	No.
Teacher:	So that's all right, so both tents have got a watch. So everybody can know that it's too early to wake and make a noise.
Alan:	Hey, the paper's . . .
Teacher:	We're not saying you can't get up, are we ? We're saying if you get up you must be quiet.
Rachel:	Can we come downstairs and get a book if we want to ?
Mrs W:	No.
Teacher:	You can take a book up with you before you go upstairs to bed.
Anthony:	Can we take a comic out ?
Teacher:	You can take a comic out to read, yes, you can take books or comics.
Beverly:	I've got a book upstairs, Mrs Lyons, (my book is called) 'The Schoolgirl's Handbook' and it's got about camping, hiking . . .
Anthony:	Oh God, here we go again. She's told us that about five times.

Marie:	Beverly . . .
Anthony:	You could go to sleep at the rate she tells it.
Michael:	Mrs Lyons, it's stopped.
Teacher:	What's stopped?
Michael:	The clock. It's a quarter to eleven.
Teacher:	Oh that is a good time. You should have been in bed two hours ago.
Michael:	Oh [*laughs.*]
Teacher:	All right, so we've decided. Before s . . . is that clear everybody? (Yes) Before seven o'clock nobody is to make a sound. Yes – um – you've got to be ready for breakfast by 8 o'clock, and we're going to have a breakfast bell.
Mrs W:	It's no good ringing the breakfast bell if the cook's overslept.
Teacher:	Oh yes. I was going to say, the meal bells you have to consult the cook before you ring it, so you . . .
Peter:	Do we have to (have) a cooked (breakfast)?
Wendy:	Who's the cook?
Mrs W:	Me. Well, I want a toast maker in that case.
Clifford:	Me.
Teacher:	Yes, well, Clifford offered to be toast maker.
Jane:	I can make toast.
Teacher:	When you've finished your breakfast, you'll have to pack your sandwiches up, so everybody back in here with tupperware containers to collect sandwiches.
Karen:	Mrs Lyons, I've eaten all my sandwiches.
Teacher:	After breakfast there'll be time to go off and get your place ship-shape. The tents are your places for sleeping in this week so it's your job to keep them . . .
Jane:	After breakfast?
Teacher:	And I think we ought to have a little inspection round before we go off, one of us'll come and have a quick inspection.
Anthony:	Me!
Marie:	Oh can I do the inspection?

42

Jane:	Oh can I ?
Mrs W:	One of *us*.
Teacher:	Is there anything else that we need to make a rule about ?
Jane:	Mmmm.
Karen:	Mrs Lyons have you told everybody about girls not going into the boys' tent and . . .
Teacher:	No we haven't talked about that.
Alan [*Talking about something quite different, probably birds' eggs*]:	He had two o' them, because I picked one up . . .
Teacher:	What's, shall we make a rule about this one ?
Children:	Yeah.
Beverly:	. . . Boys coming in when we're in awkward positions.
Teacher:	Right. No boys upstairs.
Michael:	No girls in the tents.
Beverly:	No, no girls in the tents.
Teacher:	No girls in the tents.
Marie:	Oh that's not fair.
—:	I agree with her.
Marie:	I like it in the tent.
Karen:	Boys aren't like us.
Alan:	Mrs West.
Mrs W:	Yes ?
Beverly:	Boys have got a few different points.
Alan:	We've got a nest of earwigs in the tent.
Mrs W:	Good.
Karen:	Put some ant-killer on them.
Teacher:	So if he comes jumping out like a jack in the box first thing in the morning, we'll know what's the matter with him.
—:	Who ?
Teacher:	Is that a rule ? Have we made that rule then ?
Children:	No – yes.
Beverly:	Yes, we have.
Teacher:	Are there any more rules we need to make ?
Anthony:	No. Can we go to bed now ?
Beverly:	No more.

—:	⎰	Don't be cheeky to the teacher.
Marie:	⎱	Can we go to bed now?
—:		Can we go to bed now?

5. The Aryans: John and Robin

John Guenigault and Robin Page, second year, Walworth School, are going over the work in their folders on India. Their teacher had suggested that they switched on a tape-recorder while they were going over their work. They were accustomed to recording activities of all sorts and liked to play the tapes back and discuss them. Their teacher makes his comments on their talk at the end of the transcript.

J: Got a book?

R: Books. [*Inaudible.*]

J: That's a good idea. All right, we'll read what we've put down about India.

R: Here you are. I've got an [*inaudible*].

J: Oh, that'll do. Come on. Shall I read my first bit?

R: Yes.

J: What, about religion? Then you can read the questions.

R: 'What India means to me.'

J: No, the Aryan invasion. Shall we read that? We ain't got that in the book, though, have we.

R: No, it's in our old folders.

J: I've got it in this folder.

R: I ain't.

J: Folder one.

R: I've got mine in folder two.

J: The Aryan invasion? I'll read this then.

'Origin. The Aryans were warriors. They were always fighting. They were like nomads wandering from field to field. The Aryans came from Iran. The Aryans were one of the most successful invaders to invade India.

'Way of Life. The Aryans liked dancing, drinking, singing, wrestling and chariot-racing.

44

The Aryans were big tough people who were always fighting.

'Settled life. First they went to the Indus valley and very slowly went up the Ganges valley. Then after destroying all the cities they settled down on farms.'

R: 'The Destruction of Mohenjo Daro.

'Once in Asia there were a race of people called the Aryans, and they were like nomads, because they wandered around selling things and they never had a home. They just moved on and on. One day the Aryans came to the Himalayan mountains. So they decided to go through them. They pulled their horses because they could not ride them across the mountains. They went through a famous pass called the Kyber Pass. First they were in fresh green pastures. Then the snow gradually built up. They went in between two mountains and the snow came up to their hips but it did not matter to them because they wore animal skins which kept them warm, and they had long beards and long hair and they had hair all over the place – all over them. Then they went through a snowstorm which was very bad but they coped with it. They had to go down valleys where the snow got less deeper and they went through little caves and around very narrow pathways at the sides of mountains. Then they came to the end of the Himalayas, and looked down at the Indus valley with water running through which they have never seen before, and they thought they were aliens. And one of them said, "That is not the way to live," in an apelike fashion. So they went down riding on their horses and holding their swords. A lady came out and said, "What is that strange animal?" And the man hit her with his sword and killed her. And then they went through the city killing everyone and destroying goods.

	And in the end everyone got killed and the city was demolished.'
J:	That's a good story, that is. Better than my one. My one's only a short one. And you have described the Himalayas but I in't, I've just described the er ...
R:	Yes, well, there's a part here, I've done it wrong. It goes, 'came to the Himalayan mountains. So they decided to go through them, pulled their horses ...'
J:	Well, I'll read my one now.
R:	But I read it and that different
J:	No, I'll read my one.
R:	'Cause I didn't want to spoil it.
J:	'The Aryans.

'They were huntsmen and warriors. They liked to fight. One day about a thousand men crossed the Himalayas by the Kyber Pass. Then they came across a huge town along the River Ganges. The people of the town were peace-loving people. When the Aryans saw them they said, "Let's destroy". The Aryans came down came storming down from the mountains like an avalanche. They came down to the town killing everything that moved, women and children, shouting and crying. The men tried to stop the Aryans. Blood was everywhere. People died or dying. It was a bloody battle. The people of the Mohenjo Daro had no chance against the blood-loving Aryans. People lying in the streets dead, only the Aryans lived to go round looting the houses, then burning. A day goes. Nothing is left, except dead bodies.'

R:	That's a good one.
J:	Oh, you've described more of the mountains, I've just des ... I've just done the battle.
R:	Yes, so really, we've just done about the same, because I've described the mountains and you've described the battles.

J: Yes, so in fact we both, it worked out better, didn't it.

R: Yes.

J: Well what do you think type of climate it is in India?

R: Must be all snowy on the Himalayas and when they got down there, you know, it's sunny.

J: Well, it depends, don't it, if they're right next to the Himalayas it might not be so sunny, it might be still a bit cold and wet, 'cause of the snow off the Himalayas.

R: Yes.

J: And you know, as they go, as the monsoon winds go to the Himalayas they might make the snow and it'll snow just before they get to the Himalayas.

R: Yes, and where I put the snowstorm that would be right, wouldn't it.

J: Yes.

R: It's blow all the snow up.

J: Yes.
        And not only that, it might even bring the water in from the . . . well, it depends what type of year it is, don't it, really.

R: Yes.

J: But they could have, really, because you know, the wind blows in, brings clouds in with it and then instead of falling as rain they can't 'cause it's so cold it changes into snow.

R: Yes. And er they probably lost a lot of men.

J: No, I don't think they did.

R: Going round them little pathways.

J: Oh yeah, they might have lost it there but I don't think they did in the battle because

R: No.

J: the people that they attacked were peace-loving people. They didn't know anything about war, did they. They just liked settling down and being happy and everything.

R:	Yes.
J:	Well, what else shall we read, shall we read . . . oh I've read that.
R:	Where did they come from? I've put they come from Asia.
J:	No, Iran.
R:	Oh. I put Asia.
J:	Well, Asia is in – er, Iran is in Asia.
R:	Yes.
J:	Asia is a continent, Iran is a part of the continent.
R:	Yes, they had er. They started off the horses in India. All the people in India didn't know about horses.
J:	Yes, they might have, mightn't they. Or, the British might have done it when they went over there. 'Cause they might of, you know, the Aryans just might have left without nothing – just left.
R:	Yes, the Aryans brought the horses first.
J:	Yes, they might have, but they might not have left them there to breed.
R:	Er.
J:	Hold it. Read the questions that we've got here.
R:	Questions.

The class has been taught about the monsoons, which for part of the year bring moisture-laden air in from the sea. When the monsoon hits the Himalayas, the air is forced to rise, the water vapour is cooled and condenses, and rain or snow falls.

The passage which interests me is where John takes this piece of raw technical knowledge and tries it out. Applied to the question of what the climate would be like as you came over the Himalayas and down into the valleys, it works. The language he is using is almost entirely that of informal conversation – indicators are *well*, *don't it*, *a bit cold*, *you know*, *really*, *they could have*. What is unusual is that he is using this language to speculate about a knowledge which is normally so strongly associated with schools (as against real life) that it is almost a cliché example of arid textbook knowledge.

I said the language was *almost* entirely that of informal conversation. But this question (by John) doesn't seem to be the sort of thing you say in conversation: 'Well what do you think type of climate it is in India?' He's introducing a topic, one which hasn't been discussed, because he thinks it's something that ought to be covered and he finds it interesting. He's gently inviting Robin to set out a field of knowledge, almost as an object in itself, and this is a sort of activity which isn't on the agendas of ordinary conversations between twelve-year-olds. When he asks the question you can tell from his tone of voice that he isn't playing at being a teacher or an interviewer. It really seems as if John has so accepted the validity of what, to most people, is a strictly *educational* activity that he is able to put it on the agenda of a conversation, and then conduct the conversation in the language of conversation and not the language of 'geographical discourse'.

How is it he can talk about the climate of India like this? Here we can only speculate. It may be that John is unusual. I suspect that Robin might feel a bit awkward starting talking about monsoons out of the blue; in his world, that may not be one of the things you can unselfconsciously do when sitting alone with a friend. I think it helps John to talk in a *personal* way about the climate when Robin changes the issue slightly to how climate would affect the men in their stories: you can talk personally about experiences people might have, even if the people are fictional or remote.

If your language of everyday informal interaction can carry ideas from the world of formal education, doesn't that vastly increase your power to benefit from the educational process? How can we operate on educational ideas and on children's language to get the former included in the set of meanings carried by the latter?

6. The Beatles: John, Robin, Mark and Clive

John, Robin and Mark asked for a tape-recorder and tape. The teacher agreed and they went off to a room which was empty except for Clive (same class), who was supposed to be working. He joins in from time to time. The tape lasts forty minutes, so only excerpts can be given.

John:	Me, Mark and Robin are going to talk about the Beatles, what they are and what they will be in the future and how they started.
Mark:	First, the Beatles were not called the Beatles. They were called the Quarrymen. Then John started the group. Paul come into it after seven months and then they started as John and the Quarrymen.
John:	But then . . . then they played in nightclubs with some other two people. And then George Harrison started with them. Then in 1961 Brian Epstein joined. After that Brian Epstein said to them that they need a drummer so they got Ringo Starr whose real name is . . .
Mark:	Richard Starkie.
John:	Go on.
Mark:	Wait. The first record was 'Tell Me Why'.
John:	It wasn't.
Mark:	It was.
John:	No it weren't.
Robin:	It wasn't.
John:	It was . . . the first LP was 'Please Please Me'.
Mark:	Yes, the first LP was 'Please Please Me'. [*Sotto voce*] Sorry, I didn't know about that.
Robin:	And the second one was
John:	er
Mark:	Look in the book.
John:	Oh it's not – 'She Loves You' was the second one.
Mark [*sings*]:	'She loves you, yeah yeah yeah'
John:	But er . . . oh, blow that.
Robin:	er
Mark:	What was that one, 'I'll buy you a diamond ring one day'
Clive:	'If I fell in love with you'
John:	No, that weren't it.
Robin:	No.
Clive:	'If I fell in love with you'
John:	No, that weren't it, that's on the 'Hard Days Night' LP.

Robin:	Oh
Mark:	Er what was it, I can't think of it.
Clive:	Oh, blow.
John:	Well, leave that.
Robin:	Here, what do you think their best record was?
John:	Oh Rob, hold it, we ain't hardly talked about anything yet. You bring up the best record. We've only started out with the first LP. The Beatles have already made er four films. One was a cartoon film called 'Yellow Submarine'. That was their most recent one. One they made for television which was 'Magical Mystery Tour', which they also made a EP about, and er they made two long feature films
Mark: ⎫ John: ⎬ ⎭	'Help' and 'A Hard Day's Night' 'A Hard Day's Night' and 'Help'
John:	And also they made two LPs of both them films. Altogether they
Mark:	Wait. And then they became pop idols, singing everywhere in Europe and America. Fans screaming and crying for them.
John:	Come on, Rob, you say something . . . [*inaudible*] what this is
Robin:	This is supposed to be a discussion.
John:	But what is it then? . . . [*Inaudible*] . . . else
Mark:	We are discussion, we're talking about biography.
Robin:	Yes, we're not really talking about it.
John:	Yes, we are.
Robin:	We're talking into it.
Mark:	Yes, well. Well, we're talking about it after, ain't we. We got to get through how they started and then we'll discuss what they're up to the present day now, don't we. Anyway, they started like that.
John:	Yes well nowadays they
Clive:	They all had stepfathers, didn't they?
John:	Paul McCartney had a stepfather.
Clive:	Yes and
Mark:	And Paul McCartney's stepbrother is Michael McGear who's recently in the Scaffold and made

51

a hit song with [*sings*] 'We'll drinka drinka drink
to Lily the pinka . . .'

As a passage of verbal interchange between four twelve-year-olds, this
is very strange. What we might call the main business is the formal
exposition of the biography of the Beatles. This takes place in the first
four utterances (taking an utterance as everything a speaker says before
another takes over) and continues with Mark's 'The first record was
"Tell Me Why"' and his 'the first LP was "Please Please Me"' but
not in the previous utterance by John, though it is identical in word-
ing – that was a contribution to the argument which was going on in
order to establish the facts. Once they are established, Mark makes the
formal statement which is to stand. Then the exposition disappears for
a time and is resumed actually in the middle of an utterance by John
(after making a procedural point against Robin): 'The Beatles have
already made er four films.' It continues for a while, with both Mark
and John contributing; then is broken off, and reappears with Mark's
'Anyway, they started like that,' and with his last statement in this
extract.

What distinguishes these statements from the rest, and justifies the
label 'formal', is partly certain features in the language – intonation
(unfortunately not revealed in the transcript); vocabulary (*also*);
rhythm of sentences (*And then they became pop idols, singing everywhere
in Europe and America*). But more important is that these statements
are not part of the dialogue between the four boys. As I said before,
they 'stand', as if written up on tablets, and if they are acts of communication then the addressee is not a member of the group but the
world or anyone.

What enables these boys, sitting together in a small group, to speak
as if they were addressing the public at large is the presence of the
tape-recorder. It allows some of their talking to become composing,
and the composed part, which is to add up to a biographical exposition
on the Beatles, is felt to be solid and permanent while the rest of the
talk is evanescent and 'transparent' without qualities of its own and
acting merely as a neutral carrier of meaning. What Mark and John
are composing is a monologue ostensibly spoken by no one – impersonal, unexpressive – and addressed to anyone.

Maybe they choose this mode for what they want to do because they
feel that such an undertaking is not allowed for in the conventions of
everyday informal language. If what they really want is to state a series
of facts without saying anything about what the facts have got to do

with *them*, then such a feeling would be correct. But I think the public impersonal language is not only a means to their end of 'celebrating' these facts; it is part of their intention. They enjoy talking in the manner they are (like books ?). They like the rhythms of extended exposition, the magic of impersonal fact after fact after fact. (Some of the children who like school are in love with the resonances of textbook prose and hence love the knowledge it bears precisely because it is remote and strange and makes contact at no point with the world of their experience.)

These boys could not normally talk in impersonal prose with each other without feeling silly, but they can when their talk is being recorded. But quite how this works is hard to see. It's quite clear that they don't actually envisage their tape being heard by a wider audience. If they did, they would stop the tape every time they weren't sure about a fact or about the procedure they should follow. But they don't worry at all about the arguments that break out or the flustered hunting round for titles of records. But if the tape isn't for public presentation then it's hard to see how it can legitimate the speaking of impersonal monologue. Yet the reality of the exposition they are constructing seems to be felt by them so concretely that they have no fears about its being contaminated or made to look silly by the presence in the same context of informal dialogue. So secure and solid is it felt to be that pieces of interpersonal dialogue can cut through the middle of it and it still survives. For instance in Mark's 'Yes, the first LP was "Please, Please Me"' and 'Wait. And then they became pop idols . . .', the *Yes* and *Wait* are between him and John and the remainder is part of the formal exposition.

Here again dialogue leads directly into, and provides the material for, a piece of exposition, yet the latter remains very distinct:

Clive:	They all had stepfathers, didn't they ?
John:	Paul McCartney had a stepfather.
Clive:	Yes and
Mark:	And Paul McCartney's stepbrother is Michael McGear who's recently in the Scaffold and made a hit with . . .

Then Mark breaks into song – 'We'll drinka drinka drink to Lily the pinka . . .' – as he did earlier. He's got no fears at all about shattering any precariously maintained atmosphere of a formal presentation.

It looks simply as if they use impersonal language with full irony and are completely aware that they are only playing with it (this is not to say they are mocking the language as they use it – they are not).

Apparently the tape-recorder provides just enough of an excuse for them to be able to do this without losing face.

When your pretext for acting strangely or talking in a funny way is a bit shaky, the last person you want to have around is someone who doesn't see the point of what you're doing. Such a person is Robin. When he protests 'This is supposed to be a discussion' and, 'we're not really talking about it' and 'we're talking into it', it seems to me, he is showing that he isn't interested in the construction of a piece of exposition. He wants real discussion, dialogue not monologue. He feels what the others are doing is stupid, and maybe they agree to a certain extent. So no wonder they turn on him.

Mark, one of the two who want to construct the exposition, is ready, as we saw by his singing, to break off to play around. So is the other, John:

Mark:	They was always picking on Ringo because he had such a
Mark, John:	big nose.
John:	Like Mark
Mark:	and Dean. And Robin. And John. And Clive.
Robin:	And Mr Medway.

In fact, the demands of the 'main business' appear to be felt as less and less urgent as the tape goes on. Maybe it isn't a very realistic proposition and they're glad to give it up. The possibilities of ordinary peer-group interaction, while still centring on the Beatles and maintaining a tenuous thread of biographical narrative, are more attractive. They discover that a whole lot of the things they want to say about the Beatles (or perhaps *do* about them) are possible in the language of informal interaction. For instance, going over the good bits in a film is an activity well provided for in everyday discourse.

John:	In 'The Hard Day's Night' Ringo kept moaning because Paul's granddad kept taking the micky out of him.
Mark:	And the good part in the 'Hard Day's Night', the film, the way they filmed it when they was, kept going back and forward to the cop station chasing each other.
John:	Oh yes. And that ... Paul's grandfather kept starting with trouble, trying to break them up.

Mark:	Yes and when, when it come, Ringo walked out on his own like a tramp.
John:	Yes.
Mark:	So no one would notice him, and he put, he kept putting pud- his mac over a lady, a puddle for a lady to walk across
John:	Yes.
Mark:	and he put it through one and she fell right down.
Robin:	[*Laughs.*] That was funny, that.
John:	'Help' was one where Ringo was in it again, wasn't he, as a star, because his ring, he had the red ring on and he couldn't get it off. And the bloke was going to kill him if he couldn't get it off and he had to go in the shaving machine and his trousers fell down.
Robin:	Oh yes.
Mark:	Did you see that film?
Robin:	Yes.
John:	I did. I seen it four times, and the 'Hard Day's Night' five times.

And there is a mode of scandalized gossip which admirably suits certain aspects of their matter. There is a rumour the Beatles will break up – for various reasons, one of them being:

Mark:	And like John Lennon going with Yoko Ono.
John:	Yes
Mark:	and this walking about in the nude and everything
John:	staying in bed
Mark:	through the parks. Yes.
John:	three weeks and all that
Mark:	with his last hundred thousand
John:	Yeah.
Mark:	under his mattress.

The bits of impersonal biographical exposition become fewer and further between, the last recognizable one coming only half-way through the tape: 'The last Beatle record was "The Ballad of John and Yoko"' (Mark).

Part of the reason the exposition is abandoned is that almost every fact and opinion is challenged by someone – including this one of Mark's. Here it is, in its context. Part of the reason Mark introduces it here is to declare closed an argument between John and Robin. Robin, presumably now in a position to argue that the topic has been 'talked into' enough and can now be 'talked about', tries again with the line he used before.

Robin:	Yes er . . . what do you think their best record is ?
John:	Well, that's hard to pick, isn't it, because they've got a load of good records.
Robin:	I think that 'Penny Lane' was the best.
John:	I don't. That was good, yes.
Mark:	Sing it to me, Rob. Go on then, sing it.
Robin:	No.
Mark:	Go on.
John:	Come on, do a bit of talking. You're lazy, you are.
Robin:	I ain't.
John:	Me and Mark's done all the talking.
Robin:	I can't fit nothing in.
John:	Clive's done more talking than you and he ain't supposed to be doing it.
Robin:	I don't think much of the Beatles.
John:	Don't you ? I think they're the greatest group alive, they'll stay on the pop scene if you ask me.
Robin:	I ain't.
Clive:	[*Inaudible*] . . . nineteen six-, nineteen fifty-three
Robin:	growing their long hair
John:	Oh!
Robin:	[*Inaudible*] and that
John:	That's a load – why can't they, Rob ? You've got long hair, why can't they have long hair ? It don't matter about their appearance.
Robin:	No, what I mean
John:	Blow their appearance. It's the music you're listening to, isn't it ?
Clive:	(? not their appearance you're listening to, is it ?) They can go their own way.
Robin:	I know, but I just don't like them.

John:	Oh, blow you, Rob.
Mark:	The last Beatle record was 'The Ballad of John and Yoko'.
John:	Wasn't.
Clive:	No it weren't.
Mark:	'Let It Be'
John:	Wasn't. Last Beatle record? All together? was er
Clive:	'Let It Be', last.
John:	Yes, that's what I said, but you said 'Ballad of John and Yoko' and that was just by John.
Robin:	No it weren't.
Mark:	Weren't. It was the Beatles.
Clive:	[*Laughs*.]
John:	It was by John and the Beatles. It's got it on there. 'John and the Beatles'.
Robin:	Ballad of John and Yoko?
John:	By John and the Beatles, it's got.

After that, John, Mark and Clive argue about whether the Beatles will join up again.

In this section, Robin again tries to contribute and has a rough time. The language of impersonal discourse is little in evidence.

Mark:	I haven't heard much of Ringo really. I reckon he's, you know . . .
John:	He's going his own way.
Mark:	Ain't been in as much trouble as them, has he?
John:	Well, he's going his own way, he don't want the publicity, does he? Neither does George Harrison, he's only made that record.
Mark:	No he ain't had much. Bloody John Lennon he gets on your bleeding nerves
John:	Oh! He's always in the press release.
Mark:	Four eyed so-and-so, he gets on my nerves.
John:	Yes. When he was in Amsterdam.
Mark:	He wants to show s-s-s-s-s-s. Anyway, you know. [*Laughs*.]

Clive:	What's he want to show?
Robin:	What's he want to show, Mal?
Mark:	Well, he shows people that people shouldn't wear clothes and all this in the summer.
Clive:	Yes.
John:	Well, course you've got to wear clothes.
Robin:	He's trying to be a sex symbol.
Mark:	He ain't a sex symbol!
Robin:	He's trying to be . . .
Mark:	Sod it, Raquel Welch is a sex symbol.
John:	Cor yes.
Mark:	She ain't like bleeding John Lennon, is she?
Clive:	Raquel Welch, now there's someone I like.
Robin:	Well he's setting an example of sex
Mark:	She's got [*inaudible*]
John:	Oh Rob! You're all bigheaded just because they're, you're saying that word. Oh, aren't you kids . . . oh . . . sex . . . sex
Robin:	Come on then! I could say se- other things
John:	Well go on then. That's all you've said, all through this tape, i'n it
Robin:	What?
Mark:	sex sex sex sex sex sex sex [*Laughter*.]
Clive:	No – symbol
John:	Oh yeah, symbol. Sorry Rob.
Mark:	Anyway, the Beatles didn't use the cymbals, they used the drum, guitar and [*Laughter*.]

They discuss women singers. Robin says 'Oh this is getting boring.' They discuss how many records are on the Apple label. Then the teacher comes in and tells them it's time to pack up.

The way they end up talking is, I think, very like a lot of children's talk in informal setting – a lot of competitive display of expert knowledge, bits of joint reminiscence of funny incidents, choruses of agreement on shared opinions; directionless, inconclusive. From the outside it looks like the social machine twittering away on automatic (see Introduction, page 13).

7. Garbling Words: James and David

James Giltinane and David Smith, second year, Walworth School. James has read out a story. Are they playing, or is it a real argument ? – beating each other with words and finally with fists, but enjoying the conflict and their mastery of words as weapons.

David: That is too fast really. (?They'll never) understanding it.

James: Course they will. If it's fast readers, course they can understand it. I mean, it's, that is better than what you reading it, going slower and slower.

David: Yeah, but you was garbling your words, most of them.

James: How do you mean, I was garbling them ?

David: Course you was.

James: I was speaking plain English, mate.

David: Yeah, I reckon.

James: Look, that story is how you're supposed to read it.

David: Not fast like that.

James: Well, something like that, but they don't read it really slow like you, do they ?

David: Yeah, but they don't garble their words neither, do they ?

James: Course they do. Some of them do. They even read faster.

David: Yes, but when they read faster, the ones who can read, and read faster, at least they don't gobble their words.

James: I don't gobble my words.

David: Aw.

James: I pronounce them properly.

David: Yeah. What, 'properly' / mimics him / – is that how you pronounce your words ?

James: Yes.

[*Pause.*]

David:	I don't care, you gobble your words too much.
James:	I don't gobble my words. You say that and I'll hit you in a minute.
David:	Yeah, I reckon you will.
James:	Yeah, I will. Gobble my words. Take that!
David:	Take that!
James:	You!
David:	Take that!
	[*Fighting noises.*]
David:	You swine.
James:	Serves you right, anyway.
David:	Ah!

3. Inner Worlds

The next group of transcripts could provide a veritable feast for Freudians. Each contains a wealth of that freewheeling, associative language which springs from the mind's inner world, where intense feelings are given shape and form.

We expect children to feel things acutely, and to give their feelings expression. Making up impromptu stories is one of those activities through which we now know they explore their experiences and reveal their understanding of events which have deeply affected them. Story-making, in impromptu talk, is considered appropriate, even charming, in children. But it's a language activity that has a special kind of age limit, for it is not generally considered appropriate in adolescents, and is certainly not expected in adults, where it might even denote madness. *Writing* stories is quite a different matter. Writing becomes the medium through which those past the oral story-making age limit may make up fiction worlds. Is it that writing is considered more acceptable? Or does writing match the adult's thought processes more helpfully? Certainly most of us would find it quite a strain to make up a story out aloud, while we would settle with relative ease to writing one down. And how might the child's achievement of literacy change his use of talk? When children are making up stories, plays and poems out aloud perhaps they are organizing their thoughts and feelings in a way which they later outgrow. It may be that the older person's understanding of the world around him, and the sense of potency this gives him lessens his need to explore feelings and piece them together in a spoken fantasy.

We often feel that talk is somehow a freer medium than the written word. So do these spoken fantasies take an entirely free form, or do children use forms or conventions to shape them? It is interesting that, when these tapes were written down, they took the shape of one of three literary forms: poetry, narrative or drama. Whether or not the children exploited these forms on purpose is a matter for speculation. But what we can say is that the forms the talk takes is bound to help shape its content. That is, if a child begins to make up a story, she will feel constrained to include characters, and the kind of language which embellishes these characters. There will be an organizing of events towards a climax, and language appropriate to the mood of that climax. 'She ducked and she sprang – this is the Black Witch of the South – she galloped, she jumped, she even screamed with delight as she brought up Alice to her friend, the Black Witch of the North.'

To return to the speculation – how does the young child know of the construct we call a 'story', in all its complexity of plot and characters? In this transcript, 'The Black Witch of the North and the Black Witch of the South', we notice many references to other stories, some from traditional literary sources, others more contemporary, from television programmes. Everyone who reads the transcript, in fact, recognizes different sources. So this child definitely draws to some extent on what she learns from other people's story making. Are children unable to make up stories until they have been introduced to the art by others? The girl who tells this story is seven, and patently experienced in listening to stories. What about a younger child?

Josephine, in the first transcript of the section, is only three and a half. When we look at the transcript, the written down talk, we see a poem. Is this just chance, just the way the transcriber, as an adult, sought to impose a visual representation upon the talk? Or is there anything about the talk which might relate to poetry, in its rhythms, its intensities?

There is so much evidence in this transcript that this very young child is using the conventions of a poem, that it is quite fascinating to speculate whether the mind at such a tender age holds within itself certain constructs for the expression of feeling, a kind of 'syntax of the affective' to support 'the grammar of meaning'. But perhaps we should look at specific examples in Josephine's monologue:

> and so little boy was dead
> because he has this

> because a naughty policeman put a knife in him
> and all the blood was sucked out of him
> a little bit of blood was sucked out of the boy . . .

The little girl's enthusiasm for the boy's suffering (her brother), is matched by her delight in the words themselves – and she is using what are undeniably poetic devices, or, at least, devices which the oral-bard and literate poet exploits deliberately: repetition for emphasis ('little boy' occurring twice before this extract, and 'naughty policeman' occurring twice after it), alliteration for a kind of savouring of effect, 'a little bit of blood', and a definite patterning of the images between the boy, the blood, the knife, and the policeman. All this, with the impact and economy which bring about the effects of written down poetry. How is it that such a very young child can exploit these devices? It isn't very likely that she's had this kind of poetry read to her, though she may know some rhymes. There are echoes here of the baby's earliest language play – perhaps Josephine's spoken poem marks an interim stage, which will lead her on to story-making.

Meanwhile Josephine expresses her intense feelings with a controlled resonance which relates to what we recognize in the written form as poetry.

Now Jason is five, and he is probably quite sure that he is making a poem:

> I wish I was a diver, a diver, a diver,
> I wish I was a diver
> Who swam in the sea,
> And I would kill an octopus, an octopus, an octopus,
> and I would kill an octopus
> and cook it for my tea.

He is a young child showing he knows the conventions of nursery verse – is it A. A. Milne he has been hearing? Whatever his recent experience of poetry, he is quite clearly using rhyme, rhythm and repetition to give his talk a form which, though highly conventional, has a lively originality. And this is the kind of poetry which, even when written down, needs to be said aloud. We know that very young children derive tremendous pleasure from joining in, or adding words which the reader leaves off at the ends of lines.

How soon do children improvise along the patterns they meet through hearing nursery verses?

We should remember that both Jason's poem, and Josephine's, were uttered in a special rhythmic voice which a transcript cannot easily denote. However, the bardic quality is still evident in the constructs themselves – Jason's poem is almost a chant. The structure of the talk is more definable here than in any other transcript in the book – it is a particularly good opportunity to see how a structure (a pattern of conventions) can actually generate a type of content. The ideas expressed are influenced by the hidden demands of the mode. Jason's pattern is, 'First I'll say what I'd like to be, then I'll give an example of what I'd be likely to do', and he knows the poem will have an end. What could be more effective, then, than to parallel the whole poem to life's progress? As a poem inexorably ends – and in a verse chant this is particularly keenly felt – so will end the imaginary career the poem creates.

> and I would crash my aeroplane,
> and I would be dead, dead, dead,
> and I would be dead,
> and that is the end.

So we have talk as stories and as poems. And where two or more children are engaged in fantasy together – dramatic dialogue. In Catriona and Susan's play, which they have done before – a favourite game – the content is again closely dependent upon the devices which attend that form. The children have to be aware of dramatic conventions, especially of the type and degree of information which can be transmitted by dialogue, and they have a kind of contract between them to make the story go forward. Like John and Robin, in 'Roles and Models'*, they quite specifically use at least two different kinds of talk, stepping in and out of the main construct in order to help its progress:

Susan: ... pretend it was going all through the day ... all through the day [An instructional aside].

Catriana: It goes all through the night – and all through the day [A piece of dialogue].

The sound effects are similarly found side by side with the dialogue. Children, many of whom spend quite a bit of time in this

* v. page 150

64

kind of activity, must be able to sense the whole 'orchestration' of a production. Meanwhile, the contract of their friendships enables many a versatile performance. In the story about the witches, and in the poems, the activity is essentially a solitary one, each child listening to his own inner world – but here the activity is complicated by the social bond. No doubt their previous experience with this story and the model of play making, both engender the talk and give it shape to grow. Of course, we have only four transcripts of the kind of talk which belongs mainly to the fantasy world – it would be very fascinating to know if children's fantasy talk is always classifiable as a story, a poem, or a drama. Does the inner world always and inevitably use these forms for its expression?

If so, are the conventions of each form part of our innate capacity, so that as children, playing with talk, and talking in play, we can already exploit them? And are our novelists, poets and dramatists reaching back into their earlier days and, with the added skills of literacy, exploring and extending those same frameworks through which as children they talked out their fantasies?

In the section called 'Reading a Transcript' it was suggested that most of our talk is far removed from even the simplest structures shown in *these* transcripts. Of course, we have to bear in mind that soliloquies take on a particular unity which conversation between varied speakers naturally cannot have. And in the case of the two children making up their play, we have already noted the specific unifying techniques the children use, immediately making it identifiable as non-conversation. If it is, as we suggested at the start of this chapter, rare for adults to soliloquize imaginatively, how rare is it among children, or rather, how common? We recognize all these pieces as belonging typically to childhood, but are they typical of every child? Some people may feel that only a very few children have this kind of talk skill, and that these examples are relative rarities, whereas other transcripts in the book may seem more typical of the kind of talk children use. We know that most of the time children chat away in much the same way as the adults do in the pub in the very first transcript in this book, and that, proportionally speaking, only a little time is spent on these constructs, time which filters away progressively as the child gets towards adolescence and adulthood. But what we do not know is what proportion of all children use talk in the particular ways illustrated in this section, nor what the factors are which might make one child highly dependent on these modes, while others might scarcely ever use them beyond the most rudimentary forms (though let it be said that even infant soliloquies always turn out to be highly complex).

Some teachers have found that access to a tape-recorder often gives the context or stimulus which a child needs to engage in fantasy talk. This contrasts rather nicely with the idea that a tape recorder can seriously inhibit natural flows of talk – but perhaps this all helps us to see more clearly that the constructs of the kind we have in this section (though not all the children by any means were conscious of the tape-recorder) are more 'self-conscious', in the richest sense of the word. Can we perhaps presume that there are those occasions when even the youngest child deliberately exploits his language as a medium to gain those sorts of effects which media related to his other senses can also give him, in his painting, writing, and all his range of making ? It is difficult to avoid ending this preliminary piece on a questioning note, since, in reality, we still have very little access to children's fantasy talk, compared to the evidence we have of all their other artefacts.

What are the children in the following passages using talk for ? They are playing, perhaps, but not playing in the same way as the girls in the 'Mealtime Conversation'. Some kind of audience seems to be assumed in each case.

1. The Black Witch of the North and the Black Witch of the South

This story was told by a seven-year old girl who took as her starting point a picture she had done at school. She had recently seen *A Midsummer Night's Dream* on television and read the story in *Lamb's Tales*. Her older teenage sister is called Alison.

She was alone with a tape-recorder.

Girl: This is what the picture looks like. There was two witches all dressed in black, one pot where the little girl, Alice was, and one wall with spirals in – excuse me, because I meant Alison.

Once upon a time there were two witches, the Black Witch of the South and the Black Witch of the North. They both lived together in their cavern in the forest. They were very happy except for one thing. There was a girl who lived a bit further in the deep forest. And she was very pretty. Her name was Alison. She had black hair and part of it was gold and it went all the way down to her ankles. So one day both the witches met together and the Black Witch of the North, who was the leader of them both said:

'Hello, dear Witch of the North – the South – How are you eh? What have you been doing? Have you caught that girl Alice?'

'Yes I have. And do you know I put her right among with me – Ha-ha-ha!'

'Well, bring her to me at once', said the Black Witch of the North.

Along came beautiful Alice, screaming:

'Let me go, let me go!' But of course the witches wouldn't.

'Put her in the pot!' said the Black Witch of the North to the Black Witch of the South. And they did.

Then the Black Witch of the North and the Black Witch of the South both said a spell and held their magic wands over her. In the pot they put a frog, a toad, many spiders and many beetles. The spell was:

'May all the beetles in the world make Alice ugly, make Alice ugly. May all the stags in the world please make Alice ugly.'

Then they took Alice out of the pot and she was as ugly as ever. Off went Alice, very pleased because the witches did not know that she had a magic mother. So she went home to her mother and her mother changed her back again. So one day when she was walking along in the wood, picking flowers and so on, looking at the trees and looking at the sky – it was very sunny – the witches accidentally spied her from their magic brooms up in the sky. They were laughing and cracking about how they made her ugly and along she comes as pretty as she was before.

'Oh, I thought we made her ugly!' said the Black Witch of the North.

'Yes – so did I – we certainly put her in the pot and when she came out she was certainly as ugly as a stag-beetle itself', said the Black Witch of the South.

So with a gliding swoop of their brooms they went 'Whooff – sh-shh-sh –' and picked up Alice on their broom-brooms. Before either of them – before Alice could do anything at all she was up in the air on the Black Witch of the South's broomstick (broom-broom in other words). They took her back to her cavern, they put her in the pot and repeated the spell but in different words. It was a stronger spell – they needed it. Charms, charms, beautiful charms and the Black Witch of the South bashed and bashed and bashed again with a cymbal. Then lots of charms and lions and all sorts of things sprang up against Alice. She was very frightened. As well as having toads, spiders and stag-beetles and all the other things like frogs – they put in sugar and spices and flowers. And she came out as dirty as a stag beetle, as horrible as a stag beetle, that the witches were afraid of her. Then they set off to work with her spells and Alice skipped off home to her mother again. But when she went back – bad news. Her mother wouldn't make her pretty again. She'd lost all her powers. Whilst Alison was away she had tripped over and was very ill. All her illness had spread up to her head where all her power was and she couldn't do it any more.

'Oh dear!' thought Alice, and she cried and cried. 'Uhuu-uhuu' [sobs] (No – I'm doing the play)* When she was crying she suddenly heard a noise. Grrrrr . . . It was a lion. Although she didn't know it, it was one of the witch's old spells.

'I don't know where I am – I don't know what I'm doing!' thought Alice. The lion just went on growling. Her mother didn't seem to be able to see or hear it. She cried again. 'Uhuuuu . . .' But the lion wouldn't go away. [Pause.]

So she just cried and she cried and she cried. She tried to show the lion how frightened she was. Maybe it would go away. But it didn't. She was out in the lane, and the lion came up to her. (But you must remember everybody listening to this story that it was only a charm). So she ran off through the wood and this is what the witches had wanted her to do. She had fallen right into their trap. As she was running along with the lion behind her, she suddenly saw the two witches one on the broomstick in case she climbed the tree, and one on the ground in case she ran. The Black Witch of the North was on her broomstick and the Black Witch of the South was even more clever and caught her, and she was on the ground. She ducked and she sprang – this is the Black Witch of the South – she galloped, she jumped, she even screamed with delight as she brought up Alice to her friend, the Black Witch of the North. They took her back to the cavern for the third time, and they turned her into an ugly person and repeated an even stronger spell, the strongest they could find in their charm book. And so, when they made her ugly again, she just, went home and tried to make herself pretty, but she couldn't – she'd just no idea how. And as she was walking home, she saw, some fairies dancing all in a ring.

*Aside, to interrupter.

Here comes an almost correct version of The Fairies' Lullaby for Titania in *A Midsummer Night's Dream* and a re-telling of the story of her enchantment by Oberon, only it is Alison who releases the fairy queen from the spell.

She ran off to her back garden. She knew there was something special about the herb, and this was it. She ran to get the herb; she dropped it on – she dropped the juice on both the Fairy Queen's eyes. And told her: 'Awake, awake, I have saved you'. And when the Queen heard these words.

'You have saved me,' she said.

'Yes – that's what I've done,' says Alice. 'You see, a nasty little elf came, and put some pansy juice on your feet (?). He said the most horriblest spell. It went something like, 'what thou seest when thou dost wake, do it for they true love *take*'.

Alice was very surprised when she said the words, and she was even more surprised when she heard they were right. The Fairy Queen said:

'Thank you my dear – for do you know what that charm doth mean – '

'Well, I do and I don't,' said Alison.

'Well, I shall tell you, I shall tell you, for you, *my* true love's sake. You have saved me from death – something like death at any rate. It means, that when I woke, whoever the first person I saw, I would fall in love with.'

Then Alison said, 'I thought of that myself; I was waking you, and then suddenly I thought "She'll fall in love with me." So I ran into our back garden. There I have the magic herb, and I dropped the juice on your eyelids, and you were saved! I woke up and told you all about it. I don't want to be rude, but I don't want anything.'

'Ah . . . ee' said the Fairy Queen. 'You are having something whether you want it or not. It is going to be . . .' Then suddenly the Fairy Queen looked at her. 'You are an ugly little girl.'

'I know. Two witches keep on catching me and catching me and turning me ugly. What can I do?'

'I shall give you magic spells. You can't kill the witches, but it'll help you make you prettier whenever they do it. It'll only last once. I can only do things like that to other people. It's a shame, but it's all I can do.'

Alice thanked – thanked the fairy for her kindness and went on her way.

She was happy and carefree, picking flowers and looking at the sky, like she'd done when she'd fallen into the witches' trap, many weeks ago. She looked at the trees, she looked at the sky, she looked at the clouds, and was happy, but not for long. Here came the witches, the gallant witches, the dirty witches, the naughty witches.

2. Josephine's Chant

Josephine (three and a half) had an argument with her brother of five because he wanted to monopolize the tape-recorder. He was sent away and she began to chant in a high rather sing-song voice. The first part of her spiel seems to sort out her recent row with her brother particularly the following passage.

Josephine: There were no Easter eggs
for boy for boy had them at school
and so the girl came home from big school
'Cos she was big
and Mummy and Daddy said why
doesn't little boy go to school
because little boy was not very well
and so little boy was dead
because he had this
because a naughty policeman put a knife in him
and all the blood was sucked out of him
a little bit of blood was sucked out of boy
and so they made him better
and they caught the naughty policeman who did
    that

and killed the naughty policeman
[*After a pause she begins again.*]

Josephine: There once was a flower who was dead
and the flower talked
and this flower – the little mole and the green
   star*
um came out of it and took place
and so the grass was furred
the grass was high
and tall like a king.
There was a princess and a king
and a prince
the king was dead
because the prince is coming
has come to marry the princess
'cos he liked her
and the letter boxes were full of her.

3. Susan and Catriona's Play

Susan and Catriona (seven years six months) who are friends living close to each other are also concerned with the marriage of princesses. Long before they reached school age they enjoyed make-believe play together in each other's houses. What follows is an instalment of a continuous saga about a stepfather-king recorded incompletely because the make-believe events are not confined to one room or necessarily acted out close to the microphone.

The girls appear to have agreed on some dramatic conventions and make use of a dressing up box.

The girls play extra roles, indicating this by assuming various kinds of voices.

Catriona: Have you married yet?
Susan: No.
Catriona: Well – tonight there's going to be a ball, and, in that ball all the boys in the kingdom are going to come and stand in a row and you're going to pick one.

*Reference to a programme Josephine has just seen on television.

Susan: Don't suppose you've got Marc Bolan in it.

Catriona: We shall see. I don't know who they are. We'll just pick. I don't know who Marc Bolan is anyway.

Susan: Come on – better get ready.

Catriona: Yeah – better get ready.

Actors or producers here?

Susan: When is it?

Catriona: Six o'clock. And it ends at eight o'clock.

Susan: Two hours.

Catriona: No. No. No. No it ends at [*murmured dialogue*]. it goes all through the night.

Susan: No p'tend it was [*inaudible*].
No pretend it was eight o'clock. Aher . . . I know what that means.

Catriona: What?

Susan: Early bed.

Susan's or the princesses'?

Catriona: Tch-tch.
[*Inaudible mutterings.*]

Susan: Hey – pretend it was going all through the night – hey . . . [*whispers*] . . . pretend it was going all through the day . . . all through the day

Catriona [*Concurrent with the last phrase above*]: It goes all through the night – and all through the day.

Susan: Until eight o'clock

Catriona: In the morning.

Susan: We know what that's going to be – early bed.

Catriona [*Joining in the above*]: Not *this* morning but the next morning.
So it starts at six . . . DING DING DING DING DING DING. Six o'clock – come on. [*Coughs*] Pardon me dear king.

Susan: I forgot . . .

Catriona: Oh no. Look at 'im. 'e's got a wig on.
[*Babble of two voices.*]

Susan: We all have the same one you know.
                [*Concurrent with Catriona's speech.*] Not you, not
                you, not you . . .
Catriona: Look at him. A disgrace! Not you certainly! Do
                you think you're going to marry me ? You must be
                out of your wits. Go home. You've got a wig on,
                haven't you.
                Besides you trespass as *my* boy-friend, but *I* know
                you. No certainly not. I – I don't see why I should
                have to *see* you – they're all disgusting – aren't they ?
                [*Whispered conversation follows seemingly concerned
                with the problem of naming the characters.*]

To give them more reality, perhaps ?

Susan: . . . queens and princesses . . .
                My name's Princess Mary – because there was a
                Queen Mary too . . . [*in loud whispers*].
Catriona: I know – because – . . . ask the [*whisper*s.]
                Mary, I don't know what we're going to do.
Susan: I know.
Catriona: Your standby for instance – Hey he hasn't got any-
                thing on – well he has, – but nothing on the top.
                Pardon me dear King. Father haven't you got any
                respectable people around here somewhere ?
Catriona [*King*]: Of course, most of them are respectable.
Catriona: Huh – with all these few I suppose they are.
Susan: No – it's not you, nor you, nor you nor you no no
                no, no no no no no no. He's got a wig on – look!
Catriona: O – look at this! [*Concurrently with Susan*] Ten
                with wigs on – certainly not you . . . YES
Catriona: Isn't that your beloved true love ?
Susan: No.
Catriona: Oh – it was – still . . .
                Send him to jail!
Susan: No – cut off his head.
Catriona: He goes to jail and then for extra punishment his
                head gets cut off afterwards. Come on.

74

[*Sounds of violent attack.*]

Come on. Take him to jail. Lock him up. Tie him. With no food for ten weeks. Then he may have his head chopped off. Though I suppose he'll be dead already [*speculatively*].

Susan: No, no, no no no no no no no, no no no no no no

Catriona: No. No. No. [*Concurrently with Susan.*] Certainly not you.

Catriona: Pretend this is the last line and I inspect yours and you inspect mine.

[*We know from Catriona's mother that in the next phase of the drama a would-be assassin is arrested and his punishment is to be the same as that decreed for the imposter earlier. This incident took place out of the range of the tape-recorder.*]

Catriona [*Guard*]: Don't say a word. You're under a prison. You killed the King, didn't you?

Susan: Come on Simon.

Catriona: No – we just said we were the girls he threw in the dump [*reference to an earlier incident in the drama*]. He's fainted.

Catriona [*Guard*]: He's killed. D'ye hear me? Not fainted.

Susan [*Guard*]: Come on.

Catriona [*Simon*]: All right, all right.

Susan: Come on Simon. Kill him. Do one of your Chinese burns – they kill everyone.

Catriona [*Simon*]: Golly – he's stronger than usual – he's made out of wood.

Catriona [*Mark*]: Come on – I don't mind being put into jail – I like it.

Susan [*Guard*]: Well – come on.

Catriona [*Guard*]: No food for ten weeks and execution.

The girls draw on folk lore and fairy tale for this kind of material. They begin by talking of a ball and imply a betrothal but their make-believe world turns out to be tough, undemocratic and dangerous, more concerned with power and survival than love.

4. Jason, aged five: his poem

Jason, Josephine's brother, arrived for lunch with his Granny
having made up the first verse of the following poem. His Granny
was busy cooking lunch for everyone and suggested he should
record his work later. While lunch was being dished up he dic-
tated four more verses to his mother and recited the whole poem
immediately the family had finished eating.

When his Granny asked him why he died at the end he said:
'Well I'd have done all those things and I'd be very old and tired.'

Jason:

I wish I was a raindrop, a raindrop, a raindrop,
I wish I was a raindrop and lived in a cloud.
And it would be all warm, all warm, all warm
And it would be all warm and we'd have a nice
    cup of tea.

I wish I was a soldier, a soldier, a soldier
I wish I was a soldier who lived in a sentry box,
and when it was raining, raining, raining
and when it was raining
I'd go-o in it.

I wish I was a diver, a diver, a diver,
I wish I was a diver
Who swam in the sea,
And I would kill an octopus, an octopus, an
    octopus
and I would kill an octopus
and cook it for my tea.

I wish I was a sailor, a sailor, a sailor
I wish I was a sailor who put out the anchor
to keep the ship still, still, still
to keep the ship st-i-i-ll.

I wish I was a pilot, a pilot, a pilot,
I wish I was a pilot
flying in the air,
and I would crash my aeroplane,
and I would be dead, dead, dead,
and I would be dead, and that is the end.

4. Work Talk in School

Teachers and pupils ' on the subject'

In this chapter we concentrate on one situation, talk in school, and specifically talk which is deemed, by the teachers responsible, to be in aid of school learning. We are concerned to illuminate the following questions:

What kinds of talk are normally encouraged in the learning situations in school?

What is the relevance of talk? Why are some teachers concerned to encourage it?

How do lesson structures and physical situations affect the kinds of talk and learning that goes on in them?

We have four diverse examples, which vary particularly in the degree to which the teacher or the pupils are in control of the talk. In two pieces the teacher chooses the topic or material *and* directs the talk; in a third the teacher selects the material but leaves the children with it; in the fourth the pupils move about in an environment into which they have been brought by the teacher; they talk among themselves but the teacher participates from time to time.

A bit more detail about the four transcripts will help to make clear why we have included them.

Two of them represent the classical pedagogic method of Socratic questioning. In the first, a mathematics lesson, the children throw dice and the teacher by his questions gets them to think about the probability of the occurrence of different scores. In the second, an English teacher takes a class through a poem: his questions aim to help the children elucidate the meaning and workings of the poem.

However, although the methods used by the teachers in the two lessons are similar, the phenomena under investigation are very different, and readers may want to look at how effective the question-and-answer approach is in each situation. It is worth elaborating on the differences. The subject of all the talking and thinking in the maths lesson is (to put it at its lowest level) the activity of dice-throwing which has gone on in the lesson. Such an activity is potentially capable of being the starting point for any number of further operations: one might investigate the behaviour of cubes thrown in different trajectories and landing on different surfaces, or think about gambling in all its aspects, or about free will and determinism, or make up games – and so on. Our maths teacher is interested in none of these things. He has one concern: to set up in the children's minds an abstract framework in which the events – the results of the throws – may be located; so that instead of a particular result being just something that happened to happen – 'I've got a two and a four' – it is seen as the realization of one of a particular set of possibilities. This framework is in the teacher's mind from the start: he knows that is where he wants to arrive. Moreover, he knows that the knowledge the children will gain is true and can be proved and will be useful to them. He therefore has no qualms about keeping the talk on the single track and disregarding all other pursuits which may have suggested themselves in relation to dice-throwing: the 'hardness' and definiteness of the knowledge which is his end give him clear criteria for what sorts of pupil response are relevant and irrelevant.

A poem is a very different matter. It exists in its own right and was there before the lesson started; it was made in the first place for complex reasons which had nothing to do with pedagogy. It is not susceptible to the application of 'hard knowledge' in the way that dice-throwing is: true, the teacher has in his head at the start an understanding of the poem which he wants to share with his pupils, but it is neither precise nor incontrovertible (being necessarily a personal response) nor does it provide obvious criteria of what does and does not constitute a relevant response. Finally the poem itself is a rich world of its own and naturally gives rise, in a way that throwing a dice does not (or not at least so compellingly), to a wide range of individual interactions – thoughts, memories, feelings, judgements and so on.

Despite these differences, the teacher in this lesson uses the same sort of teaching method as the maths teacher. But for comparison we then have our third transcript, in which a group of children discuss *on their own* the same poem which the teacher had tackled with another group. In comparing the two we need to consider not only the quality of the final understanding reached but the sort of experiences each approach allows the participants to have along the way.

Our last piece has different points of resemblance with each of the other three. The 'subject-matter' which is receiving the attention of pupils and teacher, although in most ways quite unlike a poem, is similar in one important respect, namely that it is rich and complex and therefore invites a variety of handlings, responses, investigations and interpretations. It is in fact a wood with a stream running through it. The group and the teacher are walking about in the wood, looking at things and doing things. But this situation is also like the maths lesson, in that the teacher has some 'hard knowledge' in his head – a set of concepts and explanations which enable the features of this environment to be understood in a particular way. However, unlike the maths teacher, this teacher does not direct the talk so single-mindedly towards the one goal. The pupils talk to each other, and the teacher's talk, when he does join in, acknowledges that he is participating in a social situation as well as a learning one. The interesting thing about this tape is the lack of disjunction or discord between the two functions – both when the teacher is in the conversation and when he is not.

One might well want to ask: what have these pupils learnt? What geographical data have they acquired, what geographical insights have they achieved that could not have been offered them in a straight lecture in the classroom, from which they might have learnt more effectively, and systematically? Indeed the question raised by the whole of this section is, what sorts of things in the business of learning can children do – and best do – on their own? And, in the light of that, what then is the teacher's function?

It does appear – to anticipate – that children talking among themselves *can* advance their own understanding in important ways. Nor should we expect otherwise, given what we know about how talk keeps going as a social process and how as it goes it stimulates thinking, questioning, comparing and all the other processes that add up to learning. So a teacher who directs the talk may risk cutting off this informal and unsystematic but motivated and effective learning activity. On the other hand, there are likely to be situations where direction is in order, cases where understanding would not be reached, or only very slowly, without either the teacher's procedural control as chairman, active questioning as intellectual midwife, or direct provision of information. The maths lesson might be such a case. Teachers need of course to know which cases are suitable for which treatment, but they also need to learn how to operate subtly the middle ground between the two: how do we help children to talk when we aren't there and enable them to bring in everything they need to when we are?

1. Mathematics Lesson: class with teacher

This was an unstreamed class of eleven- to twelve-year olds in a comprehensive school in a small market town. The children who contributed to the discussion of which extracts are given here were not only those who were quick at mathematics: the teacher had skilfully and sympathetically built up a climate of acceptance which encouraged participation. It is noticeable how, even when his words occasionally express a criticism of what a child has said, his tone of voice (which cannot of course be reproduced here) conveys his interest in and valuing of the contribution.

This lesson was part of a fortnight's work concerned with the mathematical treatment of situations in which exact results cannot be predicted but in which there may be general trends. The children had done a number of experiments, tossing coins, throwing dice, and so on, and when this lesson started they already had some notion of how it is possible to say that when you throw a dice, which is uniformly weighted, a large number of times, about one-sixth of the throws will show a 1, another sixth will show a 2, and so on.

This is not a result that can be properly appreciated by learning some such statement as: 'The probability of a 1 showing when an unbiassed dice is thrown is one-sixth': practical experience, reflected on through discussion or private thought, is needed before the ideas shielding behind words like 'probability', 'unbiassed' and 'one-sixth' (as a probability-measure) can begin to be comprehended.

In this lesson the teacher was inviting the class to consider a rather more complicated situation and to begin to structure it in new ways. What happens when two dice are thrown simultaneously? What are the possible results? How shall we organize them? Each child was given a pair of dice, and was asked to throw them once.

Teacher:	I want to ask now what has happened – what is the outcome? Edward, what is your outcome?
Edward:	Six.
Teacher:	He says six. All right. Sally, what is your outcome?
Sally:	Eight.
Teacher:	Mm. Robert?
	[*Several results of this kind are offered by different children. Then the teacher says:*]
	Oh, I do wish someone would be different. Go on. Tony?
Tony:	Six and two.
Teacher:	Thank you. Ian?
Ian:	Five and four.
Teacher:	All right. Ian and Tony have said what their outcome was.
	[*He asks them to repeat their answers, and he writes these two results on the board.*]
Teacher:	So Ian says that. And Tony says that. Now let's go back to someone else. Dawn, what did you say?
Dawn:	Three and five.
Teacher:	[*with a note of warning in his voice*]: Dawn – what did you say?

Earlier in the lesson Dawn, like Sally above, had said 'eight'. Why did she change it to 'three and five'? Perhaps she thinks *the teacher prefers* the 'a and b' form?

Dawn:	Eight.

Teacher:	Eight. Right. I'll write that somewhere down here and . . . Anne, no Christine, it was. What did you say ?
Christine:	Three.
Teacher:	Three. Now – think. Two different ways of describing the outcome. Sally, could you describe *your* outcome like Tony and Ian did ?
Sally:	Yes.
Teacher:	Tell me then.
Sally:	Six and two.
Teacher:	Six and two. Er, Ian, could you describe your outcome like Christine did ?
Ian:	Er, nine.
Teacher:	What are the two different ways ? Jackie, could you sort of describe the two different ways ?
Jackie:	Er, one is adding the two numbers together.
Teacher:	One is adding the two numbers together. Yes.
Jackie:	And one is, er, you know . . .
Teacher:	Saying them ?
Jackie:	Er, saying them . . .
Sally:	Saying them separately.
Teacher:	Yes. Saying them separately. So – which is the right way ? Jane ?

Deliberate 'wrong question' – so they'll learn when it can be asked and when not ?

Jane:	Saying separately.
Teacher:	To say them separately ? That's the right one to say, is it ? Geoff ?
Geoff:	Um. Add them together.

Again this seems to be a guess at what the teacher wants. Sally's and Jane's answers didn't seem to be accepted, so it must be the other he wants.

Teacher:	You think to add them together.
Ian:	It doesn't matter.

Teacher:	Ian says it doesn't matter. Anne?
Anne:	It doesn't matter.
Teacher:	You think it doesn't matter. So there are two ways of describing the outcome. Let's begin with the pairs. Right . . .

The teacher doesn't 'decide the issue'. In fact, he wanted the children to realize that there were these two equally valid ways of looking at the results. After the children had begun to write a few of the outcomes in their notebooks, recording them now as pairs, the teacher put a new question to them.

Teacher:	So one outcome is five comma four, and another outcome is six comma two. Right? . . . Question – Catherine, perhaps you would like to, er, risk an answer? How many *different* outcomes do you think there are with two dice? . . . How many different ones?
Catherine:	Twelve.
Teacher:	Twelve different ones. Er, Chris, how many different ones do you think? Just have a guess. [*Murmurs . . .*]
Teacher:	Geoff, how many outcomes might there be?
Geoff:	Er – six.
Teacher:	Only six? Only six different outcomes. All right. Susan?
Susan:	Twelve.
Teacher:	You'd go for twelve. [*Other suggestions are offered. Eighteen. Kim says twenty-four. Sally says eight.*]
Teacher:	Eight. Now – are these guesses, or have you got an idea? Kim, how did you get twenty-four?
Kim:	I guessed it. Er – I think that, er – twelve – that means that each pair only comes once. You can, er –

Kim says it was a guess – but goes on to offer an explanation (albeit a confused one), so it wasn't a *wild* guess. Between the mindless shot in the dark and the logically complete deduction is a range of persuasions

83

that combine reason and intuition. This is the part of the thinking process that is alive, constructive and growing. Far from rejecting it as inadequate, a teacher has to receive and encourage its expression so that it can become articulated into a more and more rational argument.

Teacher: Well, keep trying.
Kim: You can have, say only one – one – each number on the dice can come only once. If – er, it's got to come more than once –
Teacher: Can you use some figures to help yourself say what you want to say?

The teacher here is not giving Kim another argument but a suggested way of expressing the argument – 'use some figures'.

Kim: You can only have – . If you have twelve the three can only come once because it – because you've got six numbers of each dice.
Teacher: Six numbers on each dice.
Kim: And then if you can – if you get another number you can use the three again.
Teacher: So you can have a three with a . . .

Now he starts to put the argument for Kim. Is he helping or not?

Kim: An eight, say, and then – no, a three with a four . . .
Teacher: Three with a four, yes.
Kim: And a three with a one.
Teacher: Yes.
Kim: A –
Teacher: Tell me some more you can have a three with.
Kim: Three with a five, three with a six. I said four. Or a two, or one.
Teacher: Can you have a three with a seven, Sally?
Sally: Oh – no.
Teacher: No – Well how many can you have a three with?
—: Six.
Teacher: There are six. You can have three – Let me start

helping you. [*Turns to the board.*] Perhaps we should use a space over here. [*He starts listing the pairs on the board and the children continue this in their books.*]

So the teacher has now moved away from Kim. Helping a pupil to work out his ideas is a delicate process, for all too easily a teacher can unwittingly turn a child's thought into his own, so that the child appears to produce an acceptable formulation but one which is really the teacher's and which leaves the child's meaning uselessly locked within him. Did this happen here? – it is not easy to be sure.

[*After they had spent some time looking at the possibilities on paper, the teacher invites them to revise their previous guesses as to the number of possible outcomes.*]

Teacher: Robert?

Robert: Thirty-six.

Teacher: Robert thinks there'll be thirty-six altogether. David?

David: Thirty-six. Six sixes.

Teacher: You think this. Why six sixes?

David: Six can be on every one.

Teacher: Six can be on every one?

David: Six goes with every number.

Teacher: Six goes with every number? Well, I've got a six with a three here. [*Pointing to the board.*] Do you mean I can have a six with a two, and a six with a one?

David: Yes.

Teacher: Well, that won't give me *many* more, will it? – Gary.

Gary: Because there's six numbers on a dice and we've got two dice. You can have a one with a two, and keep on going. One three, one four, one five, one six. Then two one, two two, –

Teacher: Did you say 'one three'?

—: We've got that already.
[*Murmurs.*]

What is on the board is 'three one'. Is that the same or isn't it? It is relevant that each child had one red dice and one yellow. The teacher was content that the question had been raised.

Instead of presenting Gary's explanation (a good one) as the model, he continues to ask for other views.

Teacher: Ian?
Ian: Twenty-four.
Teacher: Ian says 'twenty-four'.
            [*Murmurs.*]
Teacher: Hands up those who er can er agree with the
            thirty-six idea . . . Sally, would you like to try and
            explain it? David wasn't doing very well.
Sally: I'd say the same as Gary because there's a six –
Teacher: Well, try it in your own words.
Sally: Well, there's a six on both dice, and then every
            one of those numbers have got to have a six . . .
            six added to them . . . Six one, six two, . . .

The teacher proceeded to drag from Sally the details of this argument referring to the partially completed table on the board. He then summed up the reasoning . . .

Teacher: Six pairs beginning with a one and six pairs begin-
            ning with a two. So that's your way of getting
            thirty-six, is it? Is that what you were trying to
            say, David?
David: . . .
Teacher: I don't think you said it very well. You just said
            six sixes. But we've found that there are six pairs
            beginning with a three and we think there'll be six
            pairs beginning with each other number. Now
            back to Ian, please. You changed your mind and
            came back to twenty-four. How was that?
Ian: I've changed my mind. I think it's sixteen.
Teacher: Why?
Ian: Because . . . you're going to get six with one,
            aren't you?
Teacher: Six pairs beginning with a one?

Ian:	Yes. So you've got all the other numbers. Then er the two. You're only going to get four different ones because er you have the rest in the six – in the one line.
Teacher:	Keep going. Come on.
Ian:	And then so on. And then with the threes, there's only going to be three because you have all the rest in the ones before.
Teacher:	Now how many people can follow Ian's –
Ian:	And so on.
Teacher:	Ian's line. He says you can begin with the first column. There'll be six pairs in the first column. Then in the next column he thinks there'll be fewer. And then in the next column fewer still – [*Pause.*] Well now, we've used a little bit of space. We've still got a bit left. Would you like to write them out ? Either the way David and Sally were talking or the way Ian has just been talking. Whichever way you think is – is best or right.

Mathematics is not simply the display of logically impeccable arguments leading to incontrovertible facts. It is the *process* by which people come to analyse a situation, becoming aware as they do so of the nature of the assumptions they are making, of the way they define things, and of the implications of these assumptions and definitions. So far in this lesson the children had learnt no facts, arrived at no definite conclusions, solved no problems, acquired facility in no definite techniques. But they had been doing mathematics. Their talk *was* their mathematics.

The teacher was clearly making this one of the major aims of his lesson. His overt objective was to have the children see a theoretical construct of the possible outcomes of this experiment and then to see how this compared with the actual results that they would obtain when they threw the dice a large number of times. He could, of course, have explained the theory to them in five or ten minutes and then set them rolling their dice, tabulating the results, and finding that they approximated to his theoretical predictions. In this case the children would have been acting more or less as computers. The teacher would get through his syllabus more quickly, but would have denied the children most of the mathematical experience.

In a later part of the lesson we have been looking at, the children were to count the number of times that the various totals from two to twelve occurred amongst the theoretical possibilities that they had listed. They were to record this in the table which they were constructing, an outline of which the teacher was making on the board. He decided to introduce a technical term to describe this count as he wrote it on the board.

Teacher:	Now another new word – frequency, f-r-e-q-u-e-n-c-y ... Now who knows what that means ? Frequency – Who'd like to have a try as well as the two or three hands that are up ? – Frequency. Come on then, Kim.
Kim:	If it's continuous. Things carry on.
Teacher:	Where do you get that idea from ? Have you met it somewhere before ?
Kim:	... [?]
Teacher:	No, I see. Something to do with carrying on. All right. Gary ?
Gary:	It's the number of cycles a wave makes.
Teacher:	Frequency. I see. Where's that from ?
Gary:	Radio waves.
Teacher:	Radio waves. Frequency of radio waves. The number of – ?
Gary:	Cycles.
Teacher:	In – ?
Gary:	The waves.
Teacher:	Your wave.
Gary:	The number of vibrations in sound.
Teacher:	The number of vibrations of sound. Frequency. Robert ?
Robert:	I think it's 'quite often'. From 'frequent'.
Teacher:	How many people know the word 'frequent' that Robert's just mentioned ? 'Frequent'. Yes ? What do you think 'frequent' means ?
—1:	Now and then.
Teacher:	Now and then. Jackie ?
Jackie:	... [?]

Teacher:	You don't know 'frequent'? You've heard of it? I see. Edward?
Edward:	Continuous.
Teacher:	'Frequent' means 'continuous'?
Edward:	Keeps happening.
—2:	Happens often.
Teacher:	Keeps happening. Now that's what Kim said. Keeps happening. But *you* say?
—2:	Happens often.
Teacher:	Happens often. Does 'happens often' mean the same as 'keeps happening'?
—3:	No.
—4:	No. Well you know, if it's continuous it never stops.
Teacher:	Never stops? I think that's continuous, not frequent.
—5:	Does stop.
—6:	Stops and starts.
Teacher:	Stops and starts. That's frequent, is it? [*Many voices*.]
Teacher:	Robert.
Robert:	It means – well – 'quite often'.
Teacher:	*Quite* often. [*Many voices*.]
Teacher:	Now and then. – Well, there *is* rather an important difference here. Um – 'keeps on happening' and 'continuous' seem to mean slightly different from people saying it means 'often' or 'now and then'. Right? Well, I'm going to use 'frequency' to mean '*how* often does something happen'. Right. Now I want you to look at your list of outcomes here – your number pairs. How often have you got a score of two?

What was happening here? It might be argued that the teacher should have told the children at the outset what was the meaning that he was going to put to the word 'frequency', since in any case he was forced to do this at the end. The children could not offer a definition – how could they, of a word that had not been used before? Instead they brought up a number of associations with the word, most of which seemed unhelpful, and some even confusing. Of course, it may be that they would have had these associations at the back of their minds anyway; having them articulated may have allowed the teacher to point out some meanings that he was *not* attributing to the word, and this was perhaps as important for them to realize as what *was* the word's meaning.

However, it is not really surprising that even after this discussion, ending in the teacher's reasonably clear definition, the children appeared very uncertain about how they were to find the 'frequencies' in this case, even though it apparently entailed no more than counting:

Teacher: Now I want you to look at your list of outcomes here – your number-pairs. How often have you got a score of two? [*Pause.*] How often amongst these number-pairs have you got a score of two? [*Pause.*] Quickly. Christine?

Christine: Once.

Teacher: How often have you got a score of two? A *score* of two. [*Pause.*] Well, have a quick look round. You should be able to answer straightaway. Campbell?

Campbell: Once.

Teacher: Only once? Where is it?

Campbell: One, one.

Teacher: Here?

Campbell: Yes.

Teacher: Alright. I'll cross it out this way. Put a one then in the space below a score of two. And perhaps cross off that one comma one. Just neatly. Pencil perhaps . . . Now, how often have you got a score of three? [*Pause.*] How often have you got a score of three? [*Pause.*] Sean? Tony? Ann? Come *on*. [*Pause.*] How often have you got a score of three? Tony? [*Pause.*] How can you get a score of three with two dice?

Tony: Two and one.

Teacher: Two and one. Have you got that in your list somewhere?

And so it went on, the teacher having to help the children in the counting step by step. One may speculate as to the reasons that lay behind their hesitancy – possibly it was to do with the time-element which was implied in the definition (and in most of the associations) but which was absent in the application that the children were being asked to make of the word. But whatever was the cause of their doubts, it was quite apparent that a form of words had not conveyed the idea. It was only as the teacher took them through the actions that the idea embodied that they began to understand what he meant and were able to continue the count by themselves. It is a process summed up in the phrase 'learning by doing'. Having done this, would they then know what was meant by 'frequency'? They would certainly have the first rudimentary idea of it, but the concept with this word-label attached to it is a complex of knowledge rather than a single piece of information. Understanding is never complete, and one's understanding of the mathematician's term 'frequency' is not a simple matter of 'knowing what the word means'. The constellation of ideas that centre around this word grows as one applies it to varying circumstances, draws some histograms, identifies different types of frequency distribution, uses the notion of continuous as well as discrete variables, constructs various algebraic expressions for frequencies, and so on.

A word is the nucleus for an ever-growing accretion of experience.

2. Discussing a Poem: with and without the Teacher

These two situations, in which groups from the same class discussed the same poem, one group with and the other without a teacher, were set up as an experiment, with the agreement of the school, by a college of education lecturer and a fourth year BEd student. The children were twelve-years old, the class the top stream of a mixed school in London – Hollyfield school, Surbiton.

First, here is the poem they discussed. It is 'The Companion' by Yevgeny Yevtushenko, translated by Peter Levi S.J. and Robin Milner-Gulland.

She was sitting on the rough embankment,
her cape too big for her tied on slapdash
over an odd little hat with a bobble on it,
her eyes brimming with tears of hopelessness.
An occasional butterfly floated down
fluttering warm wings onto the rails.
The clinkers underfoot were deep lilac.
We got cut off from our grandmothers
while the Germans were dive-bombing the train.
Katya was her name. She was nine.
I'd no idea what I could do about her,
but doubt quickly dissolved to certainty:
I'd have to take this thing under my wing;
– girls were in some sense of the word human,
a human being couldn't just be left.
The droning in the air and the explosions
receded farther into the distance,
I touched the little girl on her elbow.
'Come on. Do you hear? What are you waiting for?'
The world was big and we were not big,
and it was tough for us to walk across it.
She had galoshes on and felt boots,
I had a pair of second-hand boots.
We forded streams and tramped across the forest;
each of my feet at every step it took
taking a smaller step inside the boot.
The child was feeble, I was certain of it.
'Boo-hoo,' she'd say. 'I'm tired,' she'd say.
She'd tire in no time I was certain of it,
but as things turned out it was me who tired.
I growled I wasn't going any further
and sat down suddenly beside the fence.
'What's the matter with you?' she said.
'Don't be so stupid! Put grass in your boots.
Do you want to eat something? Why won't you talk?

Hold this tin, this is crab.
We'll have refreshments. You small boys,
you're always pretending to be brave.'
Then out I went across the prickly stubble
marching beside her in a few minutes.
Masculine pride was muttering in my mind:
I scraped together strength and I held out
for fear of what she'd say. I even whistled.
Grass was sticking out from my tattered boots.
So on and on
we walked without thinking of rest
passing craters, passing fire,
under the rocking sky of '41
tottering crazy on its smoking columns.

2a. The first group: fifteen children with a teacher

The teacher here is actually the BEd student. This should be
borne in mind. He is *not* an experienced teacher and this transcript
is not presented in order that his professional expertise may be
critically assessed. Moreover, he does not know the group he is
teaching – this is the first time he has met them.

However, the moves he makes and the strategies he employs
are of a kind familiar to English teachers. Some of them are dic-
tated by the difficulty of handling a discussion involving a large
number of people: even half a class is a lot for this sort of exercise.
Thus it may be necessary, for instance, to repeat answers to ensure
that everyone has heard – even though this slows things down and
makes for heavy going. But more important are the moves which
result from a particular view of poetry teaching, one that holds
that the teacher's job is to bring the children gradually and
systematically closer to his own understanding of the poem. Because such a teacher takes on responsibility for initiating each
fresh stage of the discussion and responding himself to every remark, he has to work very hard and do his thinking on the run.
We should not expect such a performance to stand up to detailed
scrutiny. At the risk of sounding unkind we propose to try in our
comments to point out what is going on; but we are very aware

that in any lesson run on such lines it would be very easy to discover many inadequacies.

The teacher has read the poem and the transcript begins at the start of the discussion.

In summary, these features stand out. The communication flows entirely between teacher and pupil, and never between pupil and pupil. The teacher takes the role of an authority on the poem. The model of the lesson which the teacher has is of a methodically advancing inquiry, moving from parts to whole, consolidating every step as it goes, and ending with general statements which will encapsulate what has been learnt about the poem. But it doesn't seem like that in practice. We don't get the sense of an evolving structure, and what general statements do emerge are trite, and, moreover, invariably issue from the mouth of the teacher. Coming to understand a poem must be something other than this.

Teacher: Now the first question I wanted to ask you out of this is: Who can tell me exactly what we mean by the word 'companion'? because this is the title of the poem and it is obviously a clue. What do we think we mean by it Jonathan?

Immediately sets up a particular model of the job to be done – a sort of problem-solving.

Jonathan: friend.
Teacher: A friend, anything anybody wishes to add to this? Timothy.
Tim: It's more of an ally – he comes or he or she comes with you, not so much a friend . . . someone who's with you . . . they weren't friends, they just happened to meet because of the train.
Teacher: They just happened to meet. So they weren't friends to start with?
Tim: No.
Teacher: Now what about this comment that they weren't friends to start with: is it in any way important that they weren't friends to start with, but what

94

happened afterwards, what happened later in the poem? Did they remain not friends, or did anything happen during the poem? This is quite a difficult question, I think. Jonathan?

The question about the meaning of 'companion' has evidently been dropped – satisfactorily dealt with, forgotten or discarded because it was only meant to be a way in?

Jonathan: ... er ... the person that was mm the man speaking in this poem mm was getting a bit fed up with the child for not speaking ...

—: I think that was the other ... I think that was the other way round, I think it was the girl, *she* was getting a bit fed up with *him* because *he* wasn't doing anything you know he sat down and decided, 'well I'm fed up I'm stopping for a little while' and she said 'well put grass in your boots and get on with it' ... y'know.

Teacher: Yes, now why did she tell him to put *grass* in his boots? ... Diana, why did she tell him to put grass in his boots?

Previous question abandoned? written off? forgotten?

Diana: To help him walk.

Teacher: To help him walk. Now if you put grass in your boots *why* would you need this? Sharon?

Sharon: It keeps you warm?

Teacher: It keeps your feet warm but this was part of the ... can anybody find me a line ... look in the poem and find me a line which tells you something about his ... what was happening to his feet going

Lyn: ... 'm ... well his boots were wearing out ... they were worn out.

Teacher: ... 'm ... can you give me the actual line? There's another line that I ... See if you can find that in the poem. Nicholas.

95

Guessing what the teacher is thinking rather than jointly seeking the truth: no sense here that the children might have new things to say which might be valid.

Nicholas:	'grass was sticking out from my tattered feet'
Teacher:	There's *that* one but I want an earlier quote from the poem. [*Pause.*] Jonathan.
Jonathan:	'Taking a smaller step inside my boot'
Teacher:	Yes, what does that mean? What do you think that means? Timothy.
Timothy:	Well, the boots are too big and when he puts . . . the boot down his foot isn't completely down.
Teacher:	Yes, in other words his foot . . . the boots don't fit him.
Timothy:	No they . . .
Teacher:	So what's happening what does . . . when he says he's taking a step inside. What does this mean is happening? Gillian.
Gillian:	Well his foot is slipping up and down . . .
Teacher:	His foot's slipping up and down exactly . . .
Gillian:	it's rubbing against him making it sore.
Teacher:	Exactly that's all it is. Now let's get back to this companion . . . Katya. She was called Katya. Now what did this person *think* about Katya to start with? Can you find me any lines in the poem that tell you something about what he thinks about Katya? Christine.
Christine:	. . . Mm . . .
Teacher:	No? No . . . er . . . Lyn.
Lyn:	. . . Mm . . . he thought he ought to do something about her . . .
Teacher:	he ought . . .
Lyn:	. . . she looked hopeless
Teacher:	She looked helpless. Can you find one word that he uses in the poem to describe the girl, one adjective which he uses of Katya which the storyteller tells of . . . uses about Katya? Yes?

—:	. . . Mm . . . He says that she's human
Teacher:	She was human. There's *another* word. Can you tell me another word? Sharon.
Sharon:	Feeble.
Teacher:	Feeble. That's the word. Now if he thought she was feeble why did he think he ought to *help* her? Why did he . . . why was this important?
—:	Because . . . 'm . . . she wouldn't have been able to do anything for herself and she would have got killed.
Teacher:	She wouldn't have been able to do anything for herself.

He often does this – repeating what a child has said: giving the stamp of approval, as if passing it for consumption by the group? Confirms tendency for all their remarks to go to him rather than to each other.

	Now the important thing about this poem is all about this. Now really could she do anything for herself? Now the big question is *could* she do anything, if so what, and show me where in the poem she *does* do something for herself.
Lyn:	. . . 'm . . . when she's walking along she doesn't get tired and she can . . . she can carry on and she also makes the others carry on.
Teacher:	Well, close the book . . .

We omit a brief section of the transcript here.

	. . . you say she makes the others . . . she doesn't get so tired this is perfectly true. How many people is the poem about? Let's get this straight first of all. Tim?
Tim:	Two.
Teacher:	Two. What sex are they?
Tim:	Male and female.

Teacher:	Now, why in fact this boy whose name we don't know . . . Why do we think he tells us about this clothing in these two separate ways ? Sharon ?
Sharon:	Is it because . . . Mm . . . when you see somebody dressed . . . 'm it gives you a first impression of what they're like ?
Teacher:	That's partly it. Now . . . Robert . . .

Confirming that it is a matter of getting the right answer.

Robert:	As the cape was too big for her he couldn't see her footwear
Teacher:	You think he was just noticing
Robert:	And also as he was talking about his feet later on, well, you know, he just talked about hers . . . you know he just suddenly saw what she'd got on, and what they had to walk across so he suddenly mentioned to her, as well what she'd got on her feet
Teacher:	So he notices later on

The effect of this repeating or recapping one bit of what a child has said is to dismiss the rest of his contribution as insubstantial. It's as if the children are shouting to the teacher across a great distance and only the simplest most basic statements get through. Robert has in fact said something quite complex. It's because the teacher sees the process as one of methodically establishing the evidence bit by bit, as in a detective inquiry, as if leading up relentlessly to some momentous conclusion. Meanwhile gropings for tentative understanding *of the poem as a whole* are seen as a distraction.

Robert:	Yes
Teacher:	Yes
Robert:	When he realized what they've got to go through
Teacher:	Yes now what – um – if you were – you see they were hurrying weren't they ? obviously! Well, why were they hurrying – this is a silly question – but why were they hurrying – what were they hurrying away from ? Christine – what were they

	hurrying away from do you think? – No? – Timothy?

Timothy: If you were – just got out and in the middle of the war and – and you were in big flat swamps –

Where does he get 'big flat swamps' from? Not from the poem. Pictures of Russia?

– you wouldn't take your time – you'd want to get out

Teacher: Exactly –

Odd that he accepts this. Surely he was thinking of the danger as the reason for their haste?

– so what would you – what would you – what sort of emotion – what sort of emotion would they be experiencing – would they be feeling then? Lyn.

Standard English teacher's question – children are always asked to say what people in stories and poems are *feeling*. As here, they usually get away with just naming an emotion.

Lyn: Fear

Teacher: Fear – of course they would – they'd be frightened. Now – are they, in fact, equally frightened all the way through the poem? Are they frightened all the way through the poem to the same extent? Jonathan.

Jonathan: I think that the – er boy in the beginning, thought he was – er – much braver but – the girl has shown that she can withstand it more because – er – I think she's got a bit more – well – er – more stamina and sense really.

Teacher: Well – what – David

David: Stamina –

Teacher: More stamina – (more go)

—:   I reckon – well – he's got more guts – she's got more guts but he got – er – he has got – he hasn't

99

| | got the strength to walk but he thinks – he prob-ably has got – he's probably braver in his mind – you know – he could stand – he can probably stand the pressure of being – bombs flying about him more than she can 'cos he gives me the impression that he's older than she is – |
| Teacher: | Diana. What do you think ? – |

So the previous speaker get no response (unless an extra-verbal one). Children's apparent inarticulacy in this situation partly due to lack of normal feedback – the listener is not taking up what you say in the spirit of the dialogue but is assessing it against some notion of the right answer.

Diana:	um – maybe she's younger – she doesn't really – um – think about – um – you know, the fear so much except at the beginning.
Teacher:	Now, this is interesting – you think she doesn't think about being afraid – in other words she's just going on and not taking as much notice as he was
—:	– um –
Teacher:	Is that what you're saying – now can you – now can anybody find a time in the poem which would either support or not support what Diana has said ? Now if we're going to talk about the poem we've got to make reference to it. – Now can anybody find anything about this. Lyn?
Lyn:	'her eyes brimming with tears of hopelessness'
Teacher:	Which suggests what ?
Lyn:	Well um – that she was sort of afraid and lost
Teacher:	She was afraid and lost –

Why does he feel this paraphrase to be necessary ? Unwilling to accept without checking that they might understand the poet's way of putting it ?

– Now –

Lyn: I would have thought it was because she'd lost her grandmother –

Initiative seized by a child for the first time.

            – not because of the bombs flying round

Teacher: You think it was because she'd lost her grand-mother?

Lyn: Yes. I think that's what I'd suggest

Teacher: Because they'd been cut off – What had happened to the boy as well – he'd – what had happened to the boy?

— (1):   – er – he'd been cut off as well – that's what makes me think they're a bit of relations

— (2):   Yes

— (1):   Yes . . . can you bit?

—:   It says 'we got cut off from our grandmothers'

Teacher: Yes

—:   So – just seeing her at first sight wouldn't mean that he'd know that she got cut off from her grand-mother as well – I would think they must be re-lated in some way –

Pupils still taking it their way . . .

Teacher: But – then what about the 's' on the grandmother – you know it's plural.

—:   They must have been in the same carriage together

Teacher: Might just have come out of a train that was bombed – or something like this

. . . and leading the teacher to make a contribution as one of the group – a departure from his role

—:   But it might be

Teacher: Yes.

—:   But it might be both their grandmothers – so he

	calls them grandmothers you know – cut off from our grandmother's house – could be – could be her house
Teacher:	Well – well if it was that he would've put the word house in, wouldn't he? Now then – I think, really we've covered quite a lot that's going on.

But now he closes down this exchange with a procedural comment – a reminder that there is 'ground to cover'.

> There one of the – we've talked about the meaning of the poem and I think, in fact, – you know – I think everybody understands it fairly well – now let's talk about the poem itself – because, we've, we've got what it's all about and we've talked about it. Let's talk about the sort of things that the poet talks about, the sort of things that the poet uses. What about well – are you going to tell me something Jonathan – come on –

An odd distinction: now they've got the 'meaning' – solved the puzzle? – they can look at 'the poem itself', which is something different – evidently something about the poet's art and the form.

Jonathan:	I – I would've thought that this – it's not too well done – I would've thought – I could imagine it as being done by – say – a school child. Not by a proper poet – because –
Teacher:	This particular poem?
Jonathan:	Yes – It doesn't seem particularly good to me.
Teacher:	It doesn't seem good – all right. Now let's think of one problem. Which nationality did we say this was written by, what nationality?
—:	Russian.
Teacher:	He was a Russian so what difficulty does that add straight away to making it a good poem for an English audience?

Jonathan:	Well – his native tongue isn't English, he doesn't know how to explain it properly.
Teacher:	Exactly. So do you think he wrote this poem in English?
Jonathan:	No – I didn't –
Teacher:	What do you think he wrote it in?
Jonathan:	Russian.
Teacher:	He wrote it in Russian so what's had to happen to this – in the meantime – ?
Jonathan:	It has to be translated into English which does change it quite a bit – which does change the order of it.
Teacher:	It probably changes it quite a lot. It changes –
Jonathan:	As in Russian it would probably rhyme a bit and it would probably change the whole idea. Of – you know – the way it's said.
Teacher:	That's quite a good point, I think, so does this make you feel – does this make you react – does this make you think about the poem in any different way from the way you would think about an English poem?
Jonathan:	No – not particularly.
Teacher:	So – so you're – I mean you're still going to be as hard – as strict on him as you would be on an English poet – are you?
Jonathan:	Yes – well – you see – I don't see, I think this probably was very good in Russian – but I don't think much of poems, anyway.
Teacher:	All right. Well now let's, let's not bother about that – let's talk about some of the – or – let's not pursue that – let's talk about some of the things that he talks about to describe, the sort of, sequence of events – as he does – . Now what in fact does he use – some of the things that he uses – the devices that he uses – Robert?
Robert:	Well he uses – the devices – oh he uses – oh – 'walking, walking through forded streams' – 'tramping across forests' and 'under the rocking

	skies' and 'passing craters' and 'passing fire'.
Teacher:	These are some of the things he describes – aren't they ?
Robert:	Yes and 'prickly stubble'
Teacher:	Well what sort of things do 'prickly stubble' summon up in your mind when you're thinking about this and remembering the people involved – David ?
David:	Burnt grass
Teacher:	Yes – but what about – let's think not about the ground and everything else that they're trampling on – what about Katya and the boy ? What effect does it have to talk to us about prickly stubble ? What does it make us think of in relation to them as – as it affects them ? What is the prickly stubble likely to do to Katya and the boy ? Diana ?
David:	Make them stumble.
Teacher:	It's likely to make them stumble. Why is it particularly likely to be difficult because of what we've been told in the poem about them. I mean – what difficulty are they facing – what problem have they to walking easily ? Lyn ?
Lyn:	Umm – oh – what problem have they to walking easily –
Teacher:	Yes.
Lyn:	Umm – well the ground's all very rough and bumpy and they – by the sounds of it neither of them have got very comfortable shoes on –
Teacher:	– now what about the size of the countryside suppose you were to paint a picture of this and you imagined this countryside how would you try and depict this area of country in which they were involved ? Anybody any – I mean – if you – sort of – well looking at something like this how would you try and think of this or try and convey this to somebody else by a picture ? Gillian – any idea ?
Gillian:	Well – it's deserted and – sort of dark
Teacher:	What about the size of it. I think it's – it's –

Gillian:	Oh it's a wide sort of expanse of ground and –
Teacher:	A wide expanse of ground. What do you think? You disagree Jonathan.
Jonathan:	I don't think it's a wide expanse of ground because wide expanses of ground often tend to have not bumpy surfaces.

An interesting generalization! But the next bit is enactive, visualizing – the sort of thing they need to be doing?

	I think it's been all squashed together and there's lots of barbed wire round and they have to trample over so much and they're getting so tired over a little space of – eh – eh – length of walk.
Teacher:	All right. Paul – what do you think?
Paul:	Umm – somebody said something about being deserted. I wouldn't say deserted because, I mean, it's in the middle of an air raid, isn't it.
Teacher:	Yes.
Paul:	And there must be other people running away from it as well
Teacher:	Yes – Yes – Yes but – so there are probably other people – but would these two, would Katya and the boy, be aware of these other people – Sharon?
Sharon:	I don't think they would bc. I think they would be concerned with themselves.
Teacher:	Yes – now – But why do you think this? Can you – anybody – why do you think
Sharon:	I –
Teacher:	Umm –
Sharon:	I don't really know – but – they do seem – [*inaudible*]
Teacher:	Is it just an impression you get from the poem?
Sharon:	Yes.
Teacher:	Robert.
Robert:	I think anyone would think of themselves in a situation like this and not think
Teacher:	Why because it's –

Robert: about other people because a boy of say – I sup-
            pose he must be about – fourteen – quite prob-
            ably – and the girl nine – well, they wouldn't think
            of other people running about, they'd think, well
            they can look after themselves, we must go on with
            our tramp – you know

Teacher: Do you think it's necessarily because they're the
            age they are or because they're generally in this
            situation that they're in one so difficult?

Robert: Well, for a start I think it's mainly because of their
            age because they're, they're quite young con-
            sidering all the other people that must be running
            about – except for the two little ones with the older
            ones. But they're by themselves so they've got to
            think of themselves

Teacher: They've got to think of themselves –

Robert: Yes – otherwise if they think of other people you
            know they're likely to get themselves left behind –
            and also I don't think this is done in Russia – I
            don't think they're talking about Russia

Teacher: Don't you. Why?

Robert: Well. I would have – I would have thought Russia
            flat land, hardly any streams and probably snow-
            ing – I always think of Russia as full of snow –
            covered with snow

Teacher: It's not always – actually

Robert: Yes but – [*Teacher murmurs.*] Anyway the Ger-
            mans didn't start dive bombing Russia, did they,
            until forty-two

Teacher: Yes they were bombing – this is in fact, Russia.
            But it's not terribly important – Timothy –

Not important – to whom?

Tim: Well, the whole thing now connected with the
            thing – I –

The real thing again. How far is the sort of operation that Tim performs with success – working from his imaginative understanding of the situation in the poem – one that this sort of teaching gives scope for?

> I picture it as you know these old-fashioned battles with their big tanks coming at each other. I picture it like one of those afterwards – a big flat waste land with – craters around – bomb craters – fire, a few arms lying around, maybe a few dead bodies and – I – lots of people fleeing and I suggest – I don't seem to picture other people only picture seeing these two in a vast expanse of land by themselves, away from everything even though they haven't been running that long.

Teacher: You, you see them in the landscape on their own?

Tim: Yes – in the middle of nowhere –

Teacher: Yes.

—: Me – I don't agree with Timothy, there, because it says, there are forests – 'they tramped across forests'

Teacher: Yes

—: and he says – eh – eh – there isn't anything there at all

Teacher: What about – what about the sort of length of time that they were tramping. Do you get the impression of any particular length of time – in general terms – I don't mean, sort of, number of hours, but generally – Jonathan?

J: Oh – I think I've got the idea that they've got to hurry and they haven't got much length of time so they're rushing that's most probably why they are stumbling like this

Teacher: They're rushing and they're stumbling. Now they're stumbling or they're rushing about because they're frightened – aren't they. We said this, previously – Now let's get back to a question what I asked you earlier – It was this – when um, the boy describes Katya's clothing he does it in

	two stages, do you think – can you think – as well as not being able to see under her cape – do you think this has any connection with their being frightened? Can you see why he would describe the thing in two easy stages in two quite separate stages because he feels frightened – do you think so –
—:	Well, I don't think –
Teacher:	What do you think, Sharon?
Sharon:	Well. 'Cos if you're frightened you want to get away from it and you wouldn't stand there looking at the girl's clothes – you might just notice them when you were running but you wouldn't just stand there looking for them
Teacher:	Yes. Did you all hear that?
—:	Yes.
Teacher:	Good. Do you think this is a good point – [*agreeing murmur.*] Yes, I do, too – All right, now what about the sounds that are involved with this – what about the sounds that – he describes, that Yevtushenko the poet uses. Find examples – read the poem put up your hand if you can find an example of any particular sound. Gillian?
Gillian:	'under the rocking sky of '41'
Teacher:	Now. Is that a sound?
Gillian:	Yes. It suggests a sound to me . . .

A pity he didn't get her to go on.

Teacher:	It suggests a sound, that's interesting. Let's have another example of a sound.
—:	The droning in the air – the aeroplane droning. I should think that means the explosions in the background
Teacher:	These are all what sort of noises?
—:	Loud noises.
Teacher:	Loud noises connected with warfare, aren't they?

Seems to be an example of the poet's art that when writing about war he mentions loud noises connected with warfare. This investigation is constantly coming up with insights of this order – would the children find them significant discoveries?

	Can you find any examples of other noises connected with things other than warfare in the poem? Sharon. Can you?
Sharon:	I think there's fire
Teacher:	There's what?
Sharon:	Passing fire.
Teacher:	The noise of fire – does the poem suggest the noise of fire to you?
Sharon:	Where it says 'passing fire'
Teacher:	Yes – yes –
—:	Whistling – he whistled. He says 'I even whistled' and also 'the fluttering warm wings on the rails, of the butterfly'.
Teacher:	Yes.

Endorsing it as a topic which can go on the agenda.

	Now why do you think he talks about the wings of the butterfly, the sort of fluttering and the noise of the aeroplane? Why do you think the aeroplane comes into this and why do you think, well – more particularly why the noise of the butterfly, why the noise of the butterfly and the noise of the aeroplane? Lyn?
Lyn:	Because butterflies would sort of make a soft flapping noise whereas the aeroplane would make a dimmer noise – that – like it would be a contrast
Teacher:	There's a big contrast. And what is the contrast that he's making, between what two sorts of things, if you can put labels on these sort of things – they are?
—:	Very noisy and very quiet.

So Lyn's perceptive contrast, 'soft flapping' – 'dimmer', is neglected in favour of this cruder one. Even when it is clear that the child understands, he is required to make it explicit. Why? Is it to help the others?

Teacher:	That's one way of describing them – any other way?
—:	The warfare noises, the natural noises.
Teacher:	Yes. Particularly – this is the particular – so that the warfare is doing what?
—:	Much noisier, I think, more – you know – powerful
Teacher:	And it's disturbing – what?
—:	Disturbing nature
Teacher:	It's disturbing the natural order of things, isn't it? Why do you think – if we're talking about that, the last two lines or the last paragraph – 'so on and on we walked without thinking of rest, passing craters, passing fire, under the rocking sky of forty-one tottering crazy on its smoking columns.' Why do you, why do you think he uses those last two lines, there, particularly – 'tottering crazy on its smoking columns' Why do – what does 'tottering' mean – do you know this word 'tottering'. Diana – what does to totter mean?
Diana:	I – means – to totter about
Teacher:	Yes. What does to totter about mean.
—:	Well – to – er – kind of – just like – er – well. You know – like someone who is mad you know, someone who's drunk, you know – kind of a bit sloppy – falls about.
Teacher:	Does it have to be someone who's mad or drunk. I mean it's just a matter of being, what?
—:	Does this mean – getting the idea of an old man or an old woman tottering around their house with a – with a hunchback
Teacher:	If we say something totters, we can say it's –
—:	Unstable
Teacher:	Unstable or unsteady – something of this sort, isn't it. Now why does he – what does he mean by 'of forty-one' What's forty-one?
—:	Where it's got the – 'under the rocking sky of forty-one'? I feel that that means 'rocking sky'

	you know it's filled with – eh – er – aeroplanes and terrible noises and that's nothing
Teacher:	It's filled with all sorts of things, but what does it – first of all my question – Christine. What does it mean by forty-one. Why does he use this number?
Christine:	Umm – the year.
Teacher:	Yes. 1941 it's the year 1941 –
—:	Could be a sector – couldn't it – could be a sector. They had sectors divided up.

Some of them know a lot about the war. Couldn't this knowledge have been drawn on in the discussion – brought in and used?

Teacher:	Yes – that's an interesting idea, umm – what do you mean – of the Russian country was divided up into areas and they had numbers
—:	Yes – they had sector 1 and sector –
Teacher:	Yes. The only thing is – you may be right. I don't know – but what suggests that nineteen – that forty-one is the appropriate number is what, – I think it was Nicholas said earlier on that it was this – or whoever it was – that it was a fact the second world war which was 1939 – 1945, why does it – is it a common sort of thing to talk about a year 'tottering crazy' now is this a usual figure of speech, would you normally talk about a year 'tottering crazy' Christine? Is this an expression that you'd use?
Christine:	I don't think so.
Teacher:	You don't think so. If you wouldn't. I am cert – I am sure I wouldn't. It's certainly not an expression that I ever use. If it's not an expression we'd use why do you think the poet uses it? Well, if he's talking about columns – what might there be columns of, for him to write about?
—:	Smoke!
Teacher:	Smoke or what else? more – not really smoke, umm

—:	Derelict buildings
Teacher:	Derelict –
— (1):	Sort of buildings a –
— (2):	Dirt and dust
— (1):	– column
— (2):	flying about
Teacher:	Dirt and dust old buildings
—:	Funnels, big funnels
Teacher:	from what ?
— (1):	Well just any funnels, something like in Kingston – you know
— (2):	Chimneys
— (1):	Chimneys – chimney pots, you know, huge chimneys
Teacher:	If you put all these things together – you see you suggested all these things – there's the old buildings or there's chimneys or there's columns of smoke and there's columns of dirt – what does – if you put these all together what sort of effect do you get – one of – ?
—:	Dirt – a bomb site
Teacher:	a bomb site which is –
—:	Smashed up and evacuated
Teacher:	Eh – But – yes this is true
—:	Derelict
Teacher:	Derelict – that's a good word isn't it ?

Another English teacher's speciality. If only we had long enough to deal one by one with all the 'good words' . . .

> But what about the impression on somebody who is looking at this. If you were looking at this and if you were in amongst it what sort of – how would you feel about it – I mean – if instead of looking out there and seeing all these beautiful houses out there – suddenly – a sort of – aeroplane came sweeping out of the sky – how would you feel about this yourself. I mean if you were to look out

	suddenly and see that very nice white house out there a blackened mass and a load of smoke going up into the sky what would you think? How would it strike you? David?
David:	Umm – panic – fear
Teacher:	It would be panicky, but what would you think of the view you were looking at as well as your own fear
—:	Well it would be horrible horrible mess
Teacher:	It would be horrible, you would feel really – wouldn't you feel really, sad, looking at this. I mean it's all
—:	It wasn't
Teacher:	Ummm
—:	It wasn't my house
Teacher:	That wouldn't really matter, would it, or would it?
— (2):	I'd think of my own house, I think
Teacher:	You'd think
— (3):	I think, I'd wonder what my house is looking like now
Chorus of pupils:	Yes –
— (4):	Yes, I'd think it had happened to my house
Teacher:	Yes, and this would make it all the more horrible wouldn't it? or would it not?
— (4):	Yes
Teacher:	Umm – you know this sort of looking on at something and seeing this group up like this the – the smoking columns in fact – what has he done with these – with these words 'smoking columns'? He's taken this and applied it to something to which we don't usually apply a word like 'smoking columns' but I mean, a world – a year isn't propped on columns literally is it. It's a nonsensical expression – but it's because the whole thing has gone to waste – there's such a – this awful sense of waste and – as Lyn has said the whole feeling is one of being derelict. Do you know this word 'derelict'

—:	Umm –
Teacher:	Do you know it, Jonathan?
Jonathan:	Yes it means, umm –
— (1):	– a smashed up ruin
— (2):	The word just – everything – um – derelict means – um – [*laughter*] – well
Teacher:	Somebody help
— (2):	I sort of know, but
— (3):	It means there's nothing there, you know – it's a mess
Teacher:	It's a mess. It's all wasted and gone to pot – Now what about the columns. If he's talking about these columns of smoke at the end what sort of colours do you associate with this? – this is a very simple question
—:	Black
Teacher:	Black and
Chorus of Pupils:	Grey
Teacher:	Grey – Now what about the colours at the beginning of the poem. What about the colours at the beginning of the poem – One – one of these words he uses
— (1):	Lilac
— (2):	I think
Teacher:	Lilac. Come on – what colour is lilac?
—:	Mauve [*murmur.*]
Teacher:	It's a bit like the blossom on that tree there isn't it?
—:	Yes
Teacher:	It's a bit like that. Which is what sort of colour compared with the black?
—:	Pale
Teacher:	It's a – it's a
—:	clean
Teacher:	It's a delicate and it's a clean isn't it. It's a clean colour
—:	The same with the butterfly
Teacher:	And the same with the butterfly. Yes good – anything else

—:   I think when you're talking about looking outside
            and you see that house blown up – well you
            wouldn't would you – because you'd have – you
            wouldn't be never in that situation you'd know if
            it was going to happen because you – planes don't
            just come over and bomb like that, do they?

The sort of point children take very seriously. No good glossing
over it.

— (2):   Sirens
Teacher: But they did at this time – didn't they in a time of
            war – this is the truth
—:   Ah but they knew – they were expecting it weren't
            they?
Teacher: Well there's that to it. Yes this is true. But if – but
            even if you were expecting something to happen
            as you do expect unpleasant things to happen in a
            time of war, do you think it makes them any the
            less horrible when they do?
—:   I don't think you'd be here if you expected it to
            happen. You'd be underground, wouldn't you
Teacher: Well you can't spend all your time underground,
            you know, even in time of war – I mean, but this
            is –
—:   You'd hear the sirens wouldn't you so you'd get
            underground, and wouldn't be able to see it,
            would you
Teacher: Now we talked about the – now why do you think –
            let's just round this off – finish off talking about
            this poem, now. Why do you think he goes from
            the clean and delicate colours that he does at the
            beginning to this black and charred and derelict
            mess that he does at the end? Why does he do it in
            this order and why not the other way round? What,
            what's the point in doing it like this? Lyn?
Lyn: Because at first things do look brighter but then
            when the bombs have been he wants to – er –
            create a contrast between the two

Teacher:	Between – and what is the –
Lyn:	Between the clean and the dirty and it couldn't be dirty and then suddenly it go clean, but it doesn't take long for it to get messed up.
Teacher:	Yes. I think the words that we had earlier on that – I think Robert used – when he was comparing the aeroplane and the butterfly – we said the – what was the distinction we made, do you remember?
Robert:	Yes – one was warfare and the other was natural
Teacher:	So it is in fact sort of, man's making the natural order of things – unstuck.

2b. The second group: eight children without a teacher

Eight children from the same class as the first group were asked to go in a room by themselves and discuss the same poem. What follows is the transcript of their second attempt; but the first one was very short-lived – it occurred a week earlier – since they were interrupted after only a couple of minutes and had to give up.

A girl has read the poem. Now a boy opens the discussion. (He has been appointed chairman by the Headmaster.)

—:	anybody – um – have anything to say on that – to start with. Um, let's see, um – anybody any suggestions on what she means by the grass in the boots – There's a few lines on that.

Seizing on a problematical detail – something to give a way in.

—:	Well – to make him walk easily
—:	Yes.
—:	Maybe it's soft [*inaudible*] to where his boots have gone through.
—:	Yes. I think it may be his feet are too large – eh – his feet, the boots are too feet [*laughs*] are too big for his feet. It says that 'we forded streams and tramped across the forest each of my feet at every step it took taking a smaller step inside the boot'.
—:	Yes [*general*] it's –

—:   his foot just shuffling up and down inside rather like walking in shoes – um – you've picked up somewhere

—:   Yes.

—:   Um – I think this poem, you know, sort of – um – just typical of the second world war – or something like that, anyway – because – well it describes it so well.

—:   Yes. I think it's very good, actually.

A shift, here – sweeping evaluative judgements.

—:   He's got – his description's very good – um – it's, it's a little muddly but if you think long enough you can, sort of, work it out into –

—:   and if you read it –

—:   It's all sort of a vivid imagination of the whole lot.

—:   Yes.

—:   If you read it it makes sense. It's like a small story

—:   Um – brings out the sadness of the war – the child was feeling

—:   Um – um [*pause*].

Two helpful comments which everyone accepts. So a pause follows. They have moved inside two minutes from myopic attention to detail to the most general conclusions. This is how it often happens with children's discussions.

The adult reader probably assumes the boy and girl in the poem aren't related – or at least that it's immaterial whether they are or not. The children focus on this (to us) unimportant issue – but in doing so they are led to look more closely at the text, so that other issues are raised.

Somebody says, 'The actual boy himself isn't saying the poem'. The others take this up as a question of whether the poem is in the first person or not – which it obviously is, as they quickly establish. But the issue the speaker might have been getting at is whether the narrative is autobiography or fiction – and this isn't taken up.

—:   I seem to remember saying, last time, that I think the two people were related and other people seemed to think that – um – that they didn't know each other – two characters being talked about in this poem.

—: I think they know each other but I don't – they might have been related. You can't really tell.

—: No [*general*] –

—: I don't think they –

—: or he might have just come up with – you know –

—: I don't think –

—: Just sort of seen her there.

—: in the war. They got to know one another.

—: Yes

—: 'Katya was her name. She was nine'. Well, if it – her sister – if it was her sister [*murmur*] he would say 'my sister, Katya was nine' – wouldn't he?

Argument *against* the boy and girl being related.

—: No, but the actual boy, himself, isn't saying the poem – isn't writing the poem.

Not first-person *or* not autobiographical?

—: Oh!

—: No!

—: Somebody else

—: somebody else

—: Yes.

Issue dropped (but taken up again later).

—: I shouldn't think they're either – sort of – you know, distantly related

—: or just friends.

—: Well the phrase 'You small boys, you're always pretending to be brave' – I think that's a typical thing to say – a sister to say to a brother.

Argument for their being related. Deploying own knowledge of people.

—: Yes.

—: and also 'grandmothers' – well – it might mean they're different but it does seem to have some connection together.

—: Yes.

—: our grandmothers

—: Yes.

—: I don't know. It says here 'I touched the little girl on her elbow'.

    He would have said – he touched his sister – or his cousin or something on her elbow.

—: um – yes – probably, yes.

—: Yes

—: trapped

—: Yes

—: Yes

[*Confused here – all talking together.*]

—: They were on the train and the train was, you know, – something happened to the train so they can't get to their grandmothers.

—: train was probably bombed

—: Yes.

—: says it was bombed

—: dive-bombed

—: The thing I can't make out is, how they got – if they were in the train – how did they get out before it was bombed

—: Well – well. Perhaps they heard a plane or they might have – or knew it was coming –

—: or – um – the carriages might have separated –

—: Yes.

—: and there was one part bombed and the other part –

—: The parents wanted to get the children out quickly before themselves and so they got the children out before the bombs came.

—: Yes, the part with their grandmothers in it might have been destroyed and they might have been further up the train –

—: Yes.

—: and escaped it.

—: Yes, and that was why they were on the embankment.

—: They must have been going on a journey somewhere, maybe escaping from this war.

—: But why would they be so badly dressed?

—: Well, probably, the warmest clothes, – like she had a large cape on to keep her warm – or something.

—: or maybe – or maybe they've been – um – their home had been bombed and they had no clothes [*General murmur.*]

—: they'd been evacuated.

—: I think they're just trying to get out of the place as fast as they can. [*Agreeing murmur.*]

—: Yes.

—: That's why they're walking

—: and don't know where they're going –

—: no one's going anywhere –

—: they've completely lost –

—: yes – hoping they'll get to a village soon

They're almost acting it out now – and going not by the text but by their own imaginings. So far they've been trying to get themselves into what 'actually happened' (and there is nothing yet about *why* the poet is telling us this story). If they could fruitfully have speculated any more at this point, they probably would have; as it is, one of them (the one who said earlier 'his description's very good') brings them back (like a teacher) to general statements about the poet's art.

—: I still think this poem – it's terribly well described, isn't it?

—: Mm . . .

—: you know, it describes every – it describes almost everything they're wearing and describes – you know –

—: the boy –

—: what they had to eat. He'd brought these things

—: Yes, it gives you a picture of exactly what was happening in only one page.
—: It's very well described.
—: It's more like a short story than a poem
—: It is really.
—: 'cos it doesn't really rhyme
—: Well, not all poems rhyme, do they?
—: No. Oh no.
—: [*inaudible*]
—: Yes – but you can really imagine what's going on. You can, sort of have a picture in your mind of this girl and this boy, you know, walking over the fields trying to get away.
—: Actually, he's done it very well, the description.
—: mm – you know –
—: must have been – a Russian war, as Tony said, – but you might –
—: might have been
—: No [*muddle*] it's by a Russian –
—: Yes, but Russian people can write about –
—: Yes,
—: any wars [*muddle*] – German wars – I mean you –

Typical of children's discussion – they always have to get this sort of literal consideration out of the way

—: The Russians write about – say – an English country garden –
—: Exactly, yes.
—: it doesn't mean that they live in England –
—: No, true

That part was rather desultory, but now it livens up. A girl quotes a line and effectively expresses what it evokes for her. Others catch fire and lines are quoted and savoured as the group use the poet's words to create for themselves the war-torn landscape through which the boy and girl are walking

—: **and when it says 'under the rocking sky of '41'**

	you can almost imagine the sort of – eh – you know, the search lights going up.
—:	Yes.
—:	and things like that.
—:	clouded skies
—:	Yes – um –
—:	[*Inaudible*] the bombs –
—:	Yes – um –
—:	and all the craters that would be made by bombs, you know.
—:	I like the piece 'under the rocking sky of '41 tottering crazy on its smoking columns'
—:	You can just imagine where a bomb's been. The smoke's just
—:	Yes
—:	trailing up into the air [*murmur*]

Almost *enactive* again as if describing that they see.

—:	I don't get the bit where it says 'the clinkers under foot were deep lilac'.
—:	Well, I expect it was flowers or the rubble settling all over [*tape unclear*]

Now at last, having set the scene for themselves, they proceed without pause to the important things in the poem.

—:	You can see at first he was trying to be very brave and – how he – show off – trying to show off –
—:	Yes
—:	and in the end –
—:	I'm a boy. You're not.
—:	the girl turned out to be braver –
—:	I can get further without getting worn out –

How easily they drop into the dramatizing mode.

—:	Mm –
—:	but before long he realizes she's got more courage.
—:	and got more –

—: They're both very small, obviously – very young –
—: Mm.
—: She was nine. The boy was obviously old – older.
—: Yes.
—: No. The thing is –
—: She says 'You small boys'.
—: Yes but – well – she was probably about nine or ten – but he isn't, you know, [*murmur*] – trying to be a man. She's comparing him, really, with a man because she says 'you small boys, you're always trying to be big, like men'.
—: Well – um –

It peters out a bit. So the chairman – conscientiously – gives it a prod and there follows an even more dramatic reconstruction of the panic in the train.

—: Anybody any idea of what it must have been like being actually in the train and hearing the dive bombers coming?
—: Well, I expect there was absolute panic.
—: very scared, I should imagine. [*Tape unclear*]
—: I think they just wanted to get out of the train as quickly as possible.
—: Actually what probably happened was there was so much panic the doors were –
—: Yes
—: Like sheep trying to get through a gate – ⎫ [*Tape*
—: opened or something ⎬ *un-*
—: and they were pushed out ⎭ *clear*]

Notice the strength of the motivation here: there is real straining to express the nature of the panic.

—: no order at all
—: it must have been chaos
—: That's probably why some people – you know – got killed and that.
Not so many people'd 've got killed if they'd sort of filed out.

—: No – There's people running all directions just trying to get out of the way –

—: panic and screaming get no one nowhere

—: I was just wondering, though, why these two children didn't try and get with some other grownups.

—: Yes, that's what I was thinking.

—: Well maybe, they were so frightened that they just tried to run for shelter.

—: Perhaps they knew of a house –

—: Just run anywhere

Drawing on all their knowledge of how people behave in such situations.

—: Maybe – maybe their parents would – well maybe the grown-ups were killed

—: or too old to walk with them –

—: too old to walk – especially it being grandmothers

—: Yes.

—: But in other countries they – leave their – gran – elders to die – the very old people.

A powerful theme touched on and then left: a good example of the sort of bits of submerged knowledge that surface and get vitalized in such discussions.

—: It seems down there that somehow, she got a little scared because – um – she said 'why don't you talk?' as if she wants, you know, to hear something – she's a little bit panicky about –

—: Yes.

—: her situation

—: I think they must have been evacuating them in Germany and hidden out to Russia or something [*Tape unclear.*]
Where it says 'the prickly stubble' it was probably –

—: streams and forests –

—: a sort of Russian place – you know –

—:   streams and forests –
—:   rubble in –
—:   Yes, especially the forests
—:   Yes.
—:   it is typical [*pause*].

As if reflecting for a moment on the experience they've just been through.

—:   Anyone else any ideas on that else we'll move on to the next one.

Prod from the chair ... and they're back into it again.

—:   Oh! they must, obviously, um – have got out – um – when the aeroplanes were near, because –
—:   Yes.
—:   'the droning in the air and the explosions' –

Rest of tape is slower and more thoughtful, evaluative.

—:   they must have been – very –
—:   still have been overhead and they must have hidden somewhere and then they heard them going off into the distance.
—:   where he says –
—:   must have been an air-raid shelter, I should imagine.
—:   When – he says –
—:   Yes
—:   he must take her under his wing he probably when he heard the droning of the aeroplanes he got frightened as well and he really wanted company –
—:   Yes.
—:   so he thought of an excuse, which was to go up to the little girl and – sort of – say to her, you know, well come on!
—:   She was obviously sad or – you know, when she said 'Why won't you talk?' because earlier on in

the poem it said 'her eyes brimming with tears of hopelessness', you know –

—: Yes

—: She was obviously, you know – 'Oh I'm never going to get away from this place!'

—: grandma had got killed –

—: probably left on her own –

—: I've read a book – [*inaudible*].

—: There's a book called 'Katya' and – um – it's written by a Russia –

—: a Russian –

—: yes –

—: might be

—: Yes –

—: the same thing [*inaudible*] [?he's put it in a sort of vivid . . .]

—: Heh they could – they could hardly have been brother and sister because the poem really says 'The Companion' –

—: Yes, it would say 'brother' or something, you know

This is still worrying them. They dropped the issue before, but now perhaps they feel in a better position to settle it.

—: I think they must have just been two people on the train who were evacuating and their parents had been left in the city and they were, sort of, travelling out with their grandparents who were, sort of, too old to help anything –

—: Yes.

—: in the city

—: or possibly – or they ran a different way –

—: the children were gathered together to talk among themselves and the grown-ups would go together in groups and probably when it was – eh – going to be bombed they wanted to get the children off – cos – the – grand – they weren't so worried about the old people – their lives weren't so [*inaudible*].

—: This boy didn't very much like girls because you see, he says 'they're in some sense of the word human – human'

This remark is a turning point – why does he suddenly make it now? It doesn't follow on from the previous exchange.

—: Yes.
—: 'a human being couldn't just be left'
—: Yes.
—: as if he said 'Well I may as well help her.'
—: and I think he's a bit sharp with her because he says 'Come on. Do you hear. What are you waiting for?'
—: sort of [*inaudible*] bossy
—: but I reckon he was also a little frightened – because, I think, he was, sort of, using that as an excuse to have someone to go with. Because I think anyone could be frightened in a situation like that.
—: Yes, and at the bottom it said 'I scraped together strength and I held out'.
—: Yes.
—: I think –
—: Maybe he was very hungry.
—: I think this girl was, you know, sort of very sensible. She tried not to – well –
—: She had some good ideas, you know, grass and things in his boots. She was a very sensible girl.
—: Perhaps she lived outdoors –
—: Going back to 'the child was feeble, I was certain of it: but as things turned out it was me who was tired'. Sort of hurt his pride, I should imagine.
—: Mmm –
—: If they were getting off the train in a hurry would – would they bother to take food with them?

They're concerned that the world they're creating in their minds should make sense and hang together, with nothing improbable or inappropriate.

—: No, but –

—: I expect he pulled it out of his pocket, perhaps.

—: Perhaps, yes.

—: he probably – um –

—: or they might –

—: stowed it away in his pocket for a future time.

—: Or perhaps they had rucksacks on their back or something – sort of –

—: No. It doesn't say that in the poem. It would have said in the poem.

—: Yes.

—: It just says –

—: It would have said a rucksack by his side or something or a heavy rucksack on his back, wouldn't it ?

—: I expect he just had something in his pocket.

—: Well. They push things like that into your pocket.

—: But it's got 'we'll have refreshments'

—: Mm [*inaudible, perhaps 'might be – How would they – '*]

—: They might have meant going to get a drink in the stream.

—: When the conversation actually starts, the bombing has ceased. Where it says before-hand 'the droning in the air and the explosions receded further into the distance'.

—: Yes.

—: Actually – he's rather – clever –

—: The children aren't worried about taking shelter – because the train –

—: [*Inaudible*]

—: there's nobody being dive-bombed. The damage is now done.

—: However much there is of it.

—: All that's left is ruin, I suppose.

—: He's got quite a good idea of – of this, though. He's got – quite a, you know, good idea in the poem – theme – in a way.

—:   Think –

—:   Yes.

—:   this little boy must have been very, you know, sort of – um – sensible.

—:   Well he's –

—:   He seems to march everywhere, you know

—:   sensible and telling him what to do. Only you know, not in a stern way

—:   No. He probably felt very ashamed

—:   You'd think – yes

—:   and at the end – he thought 'Well I must try and keep up with her, cos if I sit down all the time I'll look a right fool.'

—:   She'll call me a softee – and that type of thing – yes.

—:   Anyway I think this – you know, a very good poem –

—:   Yes.

—:   It just describes things very well.

—:   Actually, I think the person who wrote it is very sensitive about the boy, in a way, – the way he's written it.

They now feel confident that they've seen the point of the poem.

—:   Well it might have been the poet himself.

—:   Well, perhaps it's true!

—:   Yes.

—:   It could be

—:   Maybe he was the little boy –

—:   Mmm – the theme of it –

—:   Mmmm [*murmur*].

—:   I think it's a very good poem over all, though.

With Yevtushenko's help they've entered an imaginary world in which they are now at home. The directly evaluative comments at the end seem to be made with more conviction than those at the outset, now that they've worked over the poem, expressed their enjoyment and appreciation of it and brought themselves to what they feel is a real understanding.

3. A Geography Field Trip

A teacher and his fourth year geography class (mixed) from a London comprehensive school are on a field trip near Tunbridge Wells. Donald and Wally have a portable tape recorder which is switched on: what follows is a transcript of the recording. The group are working on the bank of a river – looking at a meander, filling in a worksheet, taking photographs and so on.

So this is a hybrid situation – partly school (it's a geography lesson) and partly like a pleasant leisure activity (walking by a stream is something these people might choose to do on a Sunday afternoon): so it should be interesting to see what happens to the talk. The participants, in the continuing business of deciding what to do and what to say, might be expected to be drawing on two very different worlds of experience, that of the practice of an academic discipline and that of informal social intercourse.

It should be stressed here that we would expect the kind of talk this tape contains to differ from that of the mathematics lesson, and the 'teacher-led' discussion of the Yevtushenko poem for three important reasons. On this field trip the pupils are, understandably, scattered physically – the teacher does not have them all, simultaneously and clearly visible, in front of him; indeed at one point on the tape he is heard to ask: 'Where did Brucey boy and Frances go ?' Moreover, the pupils are occupied with different tasks – not all pursuing the same inquiry into one mathematical concept or the meaning of one poem. So the physical situation of this 'lesson' is itself infinitely less formal than that of the other lessons transcribed in this section of the book, and is therefore likely to permit and promote an appropriate informality in the procedures and language the pupils use. It is apparent, too, that this particular teacher knows his pupils and has established with them an informal relationship that is also likely to affect what they say, how much they say, and how they say it. The bounds of the 'acceptable' are considerably wider than they might be with other teachers. One might conjecture that this teacher, certainly, would subscribe to the views expressed in our Introduction to this book (page 16): 'an over-emphasis on purposive talk must necessarily militate against relaxed talk and the opportunities this offers for the growth of self-knowledge' (and one might add here simply 'knowledge').

The specific things we would want to be watching for in this transcript relate to two sets of questions. First: when the pupils 'talk geography' and attend in their talk to geographical matters they have been asked to investigate, how *continuous* is this talk with the talk they use for the pleasure of social contact and the maintenance of group solidarity? Do they sound like different people then, as if talking an alien language? Are the two sorts of preoccupation – scientific and social – incompatible? Can we find in the talk a clear dividing line between the two? Is the *social* talk here, as in many classrooms, even when it is permitted, felt to be diversionary – a relaxation or even a skive from the work? Or does the 'educational' topic become to some extent the content of the social exchange?

Second: how in this situation do pupils and teacher talk to each other? For example: in our two other transcripts which include a teacher, the teacher asks a lot of questions. Very often he already knows the answers to the questions he is asking – so that he isn't seeking information but posing problems he feels the pupils will benefit by tackling, or he is checking that they have understood a point. What then is the place of questions in the educational process in *this* transcript? Who asks them and with what purpose? Again: a field trip is an outing and (unless something or someone – like a miserable teacher – contrives to prevent it) is a matey and convivial occasion. If the teacher partakes of this spirit at all, does it get in the way of his instructional function? This is, after all, a situation where he definitely knows things they don't: does his knowledge get over to them, and if so, given a context less conducive than the classroom to lecturing or extended Socratic questioning, *how* does it?

By way of a first attempt at an answer, we should like to suggest the following:

1. The teacher has communicated his own pleasure in 'geography' and the activities its study involves. This is an important part of his 'knowledge'. The pupils appear to be

enjoying themselves. Of course, most of us are likely to enjoy a day in the country more than a day in the classroom, but their enjoyment does not appear to be 'irresponsible', and unrelated to the work-task set.

Donald: Isn't half cut in a lot there, isn't it the water – look Wal cut right into the inside.

Donald: Look the bank's all soft isn't it?
Look at that there it's terrific there look – isn't half a good view of some – is that chalk there sir look.

The place, the weather, the task set, the way the task has been set, the freedom to gossip and laugh as well as work, all have made their contribution to promoting in these pupils pleasure in a learning situation, pleasure in work.

2. The teacher is encouraging an active and self-reliant approach to study, a reflection of his own approach and that of all serious students. They are trying to work it out for themselves, they are making a positive act towards their own growth of knowledge and understanding. They are responding to the challenge of the task, and to the liberty they have been offered to do it to the best of their ability.

Donald: Don't look like clay does it – there.
Wally: No it wouldn't be wet would it if it was chalk.

And they are helping each other learn.

Donald: Show us your – what's that – arrows for – eh?
Wally: To show the flow.
Donald: What d'you mean the flow?
Wally: Well it flows down, doesn't it?

3. The teacher is there to encourage, and to confirm their findings if they want him; and, by his confirmation and commendation, to spur them to further efforts.

Donald: Sir what's that brownish soil over there – is that clay?
Mr M: It's a clayey soil.
Donald: Yes
Mr M: If you go a bit further up you'll find there's a – an exposure – a better one.

Donald [*as he writes*]: Pink sort of – clayey – clay – soil – soil what
else did you write Wal?

4. And perhaps most important of all: he allows them to partake of
his fuller adult understanding of the place of knowledge and
work in our total living. The work, the learning activity, go
hand in hand with the social. Living is not seen to be divided
into two compartments – work and pleasure; the pleasure provokes work, the work is one source of pleasure. The freedom to
experience this must surely be a major step in their total
development as students and as human beings?

A couple of other notes about the transcript. Because the talk
accompanies activity, it doesn't display the coherence when transcribed that a conversation round a table does in which the main
or sole purpose of the participants is to talk. The dialogue is inter-
mittent, speakers sometimes speak more or less to themselves,
utterances sometimes evoke actions in reply instead of more
utterances, and much of what is said only makes sense if you know
the context.

The tape was difficult to transcribe because the group was dis-
persed and at different times different people were near the tape-
recorder – apart from Donald and Wally who were all the time.
Talk which is in the background – i.e. which doesn't involve
Donald and Wally – is italicized. The teacher (Mr M.) sometimes
talks to them, sometimes to other individuals, sometimes to the
group in general. Speakers other than the three already named are
indicated only by a dash.

Donald: Isn't half cut in a lot over there, isn't it the water –
            look Wal cut right into the inside.

Language expressing some excitement, *and* describing the phenomenon.

Wally: Sir.
—:   *What's that*
Donald: Ask him Wal.
Wally: Mr Matthews.

Mr M:	. . . *yes yes but have a look at the, try and have a look at the bottom the profile – of the river – how do you draw it when you got ?*
Wally:	You just got to draw the course of the stream or the – cross-section ?
Mr M:	Well the cross-section,
—:	*Oh cut it.*
Mr M:	as well as the little plan of the meander that we've been talking about.
—:	*Oh I see.*
Mr M:	*Have a look at the speed of the water and see if*
Donald:	Do that bit there, eh ?
Wally:	Yes.
Mr M:	OK.
Donald:	Show us your – [*looking at Wally's notes*] what's that – arrows for – eh ?
Wally:	To show the flow.
Donald:	What d'you mean the flow ?
Wally:	Well it flows, doesn't it ?
Donald:	What's that ?
Wally [*reads*]:	'obstruction'
—:	[*?*]
Donald [*as he writes*]:	Obstruction.
Mr M:	*Look at the undercutting that goes on under the banks*

Donald said 'cut in a lot' 'cut right inside'. Mr M says 'under-cutting'. What they simply observe, and find words to describe, he presents as an example of a scientific category.

	remember you've got to write some descriptions about descriptions about this as well as your impressions – of meanders and what you're looking at – Now remember the last one is about the effect of vegetation on this – on this stream.
— [*reads*]:	*'In your field notebook describe an actual meander'*
—:	*Cuts it away doesn't it, so you get a (?)*
Mr M:	*Don't forget to put down – you know some idea – of – of depth and of width across here you know about*

134

	twelve feet wide or more – and how much it is that
	way – you know some idea some guide to you – so it's
	an actual meander not just some old vague sort of
	scribbling that you can draw.
—:	*You got to describe your own meander that you done.*
Mr M:	*Yes, yes what you done before, John that's it.*
—:	(?)
Mr M:	(?) You two done much talking yet ?
Donald:	Yes quite a bit.
Mr M:	Good – want to check it's going back all right then
	Don and then then you can play it back and see.
Donald:	Yes . . . sorry about
Wally:	It's gravelly
Donald:	Meanders a lot – right ?
Mr M:	*Shallow, shallow that's good very shallow – there –*
	that lands it there.

Donald [*as he writes*]: Cuts well.

Wally: Lots of vegetation.

Donald [*as he writes*]: in – to – the – banks – very low

Untechnical language – precise enough though.

Mr M:	*Can you see – the – the actual river meanders over*
	this area doesn't it – it hasn't got one course.
Donald:	Sir what's that brownish soil over there – is that
	clay ?

Pupil asking teacher.

Mr M:	It's a clayey soil.
Donald:	Yes
Mr M:	If you go a bit further up you'll find there's a – an
	exposure – a better one.

Technical term again.

—: (?)

Donald [*as he writes*]: Pink sort of – clayey – clay – soil – soil –
what else did you write Wal ?

Wally [*reads*]: 'Lot of vegetation – obstruction'.

Donald: Widest is about – it's about four foot wide at the
most, isn't it ?

Wally:	Yes.
Donald [*as he writes*]:	Four.
Mr M:	*Birch*
Donald:	What are those trees Gal* ?
Gal:	What ?
Donald:	What sort of trees are they – birch ?
Mr M:	*See whether you can find any leaves lying around.*
Donald [*as he writes*]:	Birch trees
Mr M:	Not birch – birch got a silver bark.
—:	Elm, elm.
Mr M:	No, no they're beech.
Donald:	Beech trees
—:	(?) birch
Donald [*as he writes*]:	Beech trees er . . . what else hold on I – what's what d'you write about the vegetation ?

Technical sort of word, taken from the worksheet, but now used naturally enough.

Wally:	Beech trees obstructed lot of – no hang on – leaf covering (?).
Donald [*as he writes*]:	Vegetation – scattered trees – and er – what else did you write about the vegetation – sir see this – whitish stuff here what's that – in . . .

Pupil asking teacher again.

Mr M:	More clay, it varies.
Donald:	Oh.
Mr M:	*Where did Brucey boy and Frances go ? Did they go – hang on John.* Stand in the water there give us a guide line how deep it is – where you were before (?) [*Someone's taking a photograph.*]
Donald:	What here ?
Mr M:	Yes – I only want your feet – I don't want the rest of you I only want your feet – are are are are they waterproof or are you getting wet ?
Donald:	That one is.

*Cockney abbreviation: Gal = Garry.

136

Mr M:	All right stand there like that just to give me a guide – we ain't too much light (?)
—:	*Kay do you want one of these ?*
Donald:	It's all different colours of clay there, isn't there ?
Mr M:	Yes, yes.
Mr M:	*Well take one where you get a bank – on the other side which is cut – where you get some vegetation on the top of it.*
—:	*What that there ?*
Mr M:	*Yes – have you got any controls on that or are you just er . . .*
—:	*No*
Mr M:	*Well look – stand there where you are and I'll see if you've got much light in there – 'cause some areas at the moment are a bit dark.*
—:	*Oh I'll not bother then.*
Mr M:	*No you can still get it but as long as you choose the right area.*
Donald:	Is this Galt clay – this ?

Pupil asking.

Mr M:	No this is Wadhurst clay.
Donald:	Wadhurst.
Mr M:	Like we saw in . . .
Wally:	What's that maroon stuff in it ?

Pupil asking.

Donald:	Clay.
Mr M:	Clay.
Donald:	Yes – it's all different colours of clay.
Mr M:	Well they're washed down.
Donald:	That one down there's a good one wasn't it the maroon one and all that

He is involved – not merely performing tasks.

	here's – Geoffrey Bruce sir here.
—:	Brucey.

Mr M:	That's all right so long as they're working.
Donald:	Banks cut into, Wal – it's got all the moss round the bottom there – just er – isn't half getting (?dropped ?) deep there, doesn't it ?

He's registering what he's seeing because it's surprising to him. It isn't just neutral data – it upsets his expectations.

Wally:	Yes
Donald:	It's wider and all.
Wally:	You can jump over.
	[*Ten seconds pause*]
Donald:	Look the bank's all soft isn't it ?
	[*Very fast and excitedly:*] Look at that there it's terrific there look – isn't half a good view of some – is that chalk there sir look.
Mr M:	What ?
Donald:	Don't look like clay does it – there.
Wally:	No it wouldn't be wet would it if it was chalk.
Mr M:	No, it's still a clay.
Donald:	It's still clay.
Mr M:	But you can see how much – undercutting you've got there – what you've got that tree's holding that bank up – and it goes back a lot.
Donald:	Yes.
Mr M:	That tree doesn't it – inside of it – and this gives you – some idea of – what it's like you see it's got some sandstone within the clay – that's a bit of sandstone and plenty of – high iron content – how do you know it's got a high iron content – think, look at it.

Clearly playing the 'teacher' role here. But this is one of the few points in the tape where he asks this kind of question.

Wally:	Iron – colour or something.
Mr M:	Yes – and what what about the colours ?
Wally:	Black through it.
Mr M:	No it's the the red in it.

Wally:	The red.
Mr M:	What happens to iron?
Wally:	Oh it – oxidizes it goes red.
Mr M:	Yes.
Donald:	Still got that cone Ron?
Ron:	Yes.
Donald:	It's quite a big tree isn't it – we've been standing under it all the time nearly haven't we that coniferous there – that coney forous [*Editor's attempt to represent how he says it*] ... come on let's walk further down ... there's something there's a drainage ditch down there.
—:	Want a cone Wally?
Donald:	He's got one.
Mr M:	Oh look – what are these leaves?
Donald:	Elm isn't it no
—:	(?)
Mr M:	Look – that one as well – yes well take some of them back I got a book in the coach – OK that's a beech what you've got in your hand now I know that one – I'm not sure about that one though at all – and that one's an an oak tree

Teacher doesn't know, doesn't pretend to know. Helps to establish the situation where the children can admit ignorance fearlessly and find answers from another source.

Donald:	Here this is isn't it that one there?
Mr M:	and an ash tree's like that as well – ferns you've got as well.
—:	(?)
—:	*Can you pass it up to me?*
—:	*Yes here you are.*
Mr M:	Just take the top one off of that ...
Donald:	Top bit ... cor it don't half wear your hands pushing this button down all the time
Mr M:	*You can draw them through*
—:	*Here you are, here's a cone here for you*

Donald:	Is this a V-shaped valley we're down in sir?
Mr M:	Eh?
Donald:	Is this a V-shaped valley we're in?
Mr M:	A very deep little – V-shaped valley.
Donald:	Yes.
Mr M:	(?) V-shape – that's the whole lot – then you've got a deep one – that the river's cut into.
Donald:	Yes.
—:	(?)
Mr M:	*Good, is it lichen?*
—:	*What?*
Mr M:	*I'll come and look at it, hang on.*
Donald:	It's been on all the time the tape-recorder.
—:	(?)
Donald:	Don't know
Mr M:	*I'll be over in a minute hang on*
Donald:	Here's a – here's a feather over here – wood pigeon's is it?
—:	Who am I supposed to give this to?
Donald:	Kay – come on Wal let's go
—:	He nearly pushed him in the river up there him with his tape-recorder and all.
—:	jumped it
—:	I jumped in the bloody mud
Donald:	Watch the language – tape-recorder's on ... what's she got?
Mr M:	There's a very strange I can see some more of it grows on rocks – anywhere – all different sorts it's called lichen [*spells it*] L-I-C-H-E-N like they get in tundra areas they talk about mosses and lichens don't we or lichens [*pronouncing it litchens*] maybe used
—:	Lichens [*pronouncing it litchens*].
Donald:	What is it, a moss or a fungus?
Mr M:	NO the word is lichen [*liken*] really but most people say lichens [*litchens*]. Yes.

The sort of information a teacher can give, but a peer can't?

Donald:	Is it a moss or a fungus sir?
Mr M:	Erm – it's an algae and a – a fungus – they live together – it's very strange one lives off the other one.
—:	(?)
—:	(?)
Mr M:	Yes yes that's all you want
—:	There's one of them what's a name leaves sir?
—:	O K find me a brown leaf.
Mr M:	What sort – there's all manner of sorts.
—:	(?)
Mr M:	Do you want do you want to take this – part of this?
Donald:	What's that does it rot the wood or what that
Mr M:	No it just lives off it.
Donald:	Oh I thought it rotted it.
Mr M:	Yes look there's an oak leaf here.
—:	I want an oak leaf
—:	I got a couple of them
Mr M:	Now oo now look look look look
Donald:	Acorn – want it?
Mr M:	Thank you yes.
—:	Squirrel nut
—:	Here's a good one.
Mr M:	Acorn.
—:	Oh let me have one.
—:	I'll have that one sir.
Mr M:	Another piece of evidence isn't it?

Technical attitude: for him the operation is a scientific inquiry.

—:	I'm going to put that in my pocket I might lose that.
—:	I'll draw that.
Donald:	Might be squirrels round here in hibernation and all that.
Mr M:	Might be able to press it I don't I shouldn't think so – if you (?secure?) it I'll show it to you in the book.

Donald:	Will there be squirrels about here in hibernation somewhere?
Mr M:	Yes – hibernating.
—:	There's a bird's nest over there.
—:	Oh look a bird's nest.
—:	Isn't it a big one.
Donald:	It's most probably a crow's – [*whispers*] shut your mouth [*laughs*].
Mr M:	Where's Brucey boy, has he come out of the woods yet?
Donald:	Yes.
Mr M:	Here –
—:	Humus.
Mr M:	Humus yes look and in many places it's great depth – that's very good for the garden – my old man used to make me go out in the woods – regular – this time of the year – OK – every time this time of the year armed with a big cart – my brothers and I used to be up up the woods fill the cart up with leaf mould – what we used to call leaf mould – humus – take it back for the garden – no not in the woods you don't.

The teacher adopting a very different role here.

Donald:	What is it, a sort of manure?
Mr M:	Yes well it it's very rich it's very acid and it's very good on chalk soils because chalk is alkaline – What, no it's ivy.
—:	Poisoned ivy.
Mr M:	Oh dear no – that's a record (?) – going in my day you don't mean to say they've revived it have they?
Donald:	Yes.
Mr M:	Mind how you go Wally.
Donald:	That little stream doesn't half cut into them banks – deep in some places doesn't it?
Mr M:	Yes well it's very difficult for you to think about it at the moment, now the last time when I came on

that Sunday – there was twice as much water in there.

This transcript makes an interesting comparison with the other three. The pupils talk to each other, as do the group discussing the poem on their own, to help themselves observe, interpret and understand what is there. But, unlike the poem group, they slip backwards and forwards between this and purely social talk. They are, again like that group, investigating on their own but with the difference that the teacher's knowledge is available to them when they want it: they can ask him about things, and they do. But his expertise has also impinged on them by way of his worksheet which points them in certain directions and ensures that they give attention to the features he knows to be instructive. (Worksheets can, of course, have a confining and blinkering effect; but that doesn't seem to have happened here.) The teacher on the whole answers rather than asks questions – he also gives procedural instructions – and contributes to the social as well as the academic proceedings. But the line isn't easy to draw – and this seems an index of the effectiveness of the situation. When he talks about manure, he's making a point which is 'on the subject': but isn't there just as strong an element of sharing an enjoyable reminiscence? As for the pupils, there does seem to be some continuity between the spontaneous social expression of natural curiosity about the world and the practice of the techniques of a specialist discipline, so that the latter does not here, as so often, look like the mindless performance of learnt tricks.

What do we learn from the set of four transcripts? Perhaps that the interpersonal processes of inquiry that children will, in the right set-up, get going by themselves can take them further than we usually suppose? And the teacher's contribution could more often be made 'on the run', by monitoring and coming in on a process that is basically running itself, galloping up to the advancing column and warning of indians ahead, pointing out old bones by the roadside and delivering ammunition, then withdrawing – rather than keeping the map to himself and directing each step of each individual with detachment from some nearby eminence?

5. Roles and Models

This section centres on another aspect of talk that is more than communication. We suggest that each of the transcripts that follow shows the speakers to be attempting to play a role – perhaps because this is the activity the teacher has requested or perhaps because the speaker is playing at 'grown-ups', adopting a role with its appropriate language patterns. We would not want to imply that such an activity is essentially 'childish' and that we grow out of it as we mature. All of us, some of the time, try out different roles and attempt to adopt a mode of dress, stance and behaviour, as well as language, that we feel to be mildly foreign to us. We hesitate to go any further but tentatively could one say that at such moments we may be deliberately and consciously mimicking for the entertainment of our peer; or we may be implying a momentary dissatisfaction with the role life has cast us in and saying as it were: 'I am also, potentially, a BBC reporter, an interviewer, a philosopher, a policeman, an entertainer, a beautiful girl.' We would accept that children are constantly changing roles – trying them out, as it were, in an attempt to find one that fits their needs and talents; aspiring to adult status via adult roles; and simply playing with language in an only dimly-realized attempt to extend their mastery. Wouldn't it be true to say for example that, in the transcripts that follow, (1) Alan and Karen, having been asked to recall what happened at the market, are playing (one more confidently and successfully than the other) at BBC reporter; (3) that John is playing at interviewer and Robin (again less successfully, somewhat to the mild irritation of John) at interviewee; (4) that Keith is trying hard to rise to the occasion and give a talk – perhaps the most extended utterance he had ever been allowed to make in his life – that in part is to show himself and the world that he is worthy of serious attention, an adult not a child?

We suggest that in all of these transcripts we can distinguish an element of dramatic play; that all of us, adults and children, indulge in this kind of talk-behaviour; and need opportunities to play in this way beyond the possibly critical, satirical, eye of parent, teacher or peer.

Teachers and parents have seen children disconcerted by a strange adult peering over the wall of their Wendy House, their play disrupted, and themselves brought back to the here-and-now and the limited and limiting roles the here-and-now requires of them.

Might we conjecture even that such an interruption causes temporary regression to an earlier stage of childhood – a sense of insecurity, of inadequacy in the serious world. 'There I was . . . and I felt such a fool, I don't know what he thought of me. It's safer to play the role I know he expects me to play.'

1. At the Market: Karen and Alan

The transcript that follows is an extract from field recordings made on a week away from a Bristol school in a cottage in Wales.*
The class teacher accompanied fourteen children, half of her class of mixed-ability nine-year olds, boys and girls.

Alan: Today we got up, got in the mini-bus, and went to the cattle market, and we split up and went into three groups – um – over to Karen.

Karen: Well in the Cattle Market there were lots of calves and the calves were making more noises than their mothers and fathers, and – um – everybody as we were walking past the pens, they were all going 'Baaa' and we were talking to a sheep in one of the pens, and as we said 'Baaa' he said 'Baaa'. And this is how we were. Ah, these are standing there going 'baa' and him going 'baa' and all these men were looking at us wondering what we were doing.

And suddenly this man – well – this horsebox came along, and you could tell that there were

* v. also Seven Situations 4: Rule-making page 38.

pigs in there, the stink was terrible and – um – there was this man and um – he had this great big walking stick and he was hitting the pigs on the back, so the pigs must have very hard skin because you know they were just waddling along not worrying about anything.

Both children adopt a style which they would not normally use in conversation, e.g. the careful sequence of Alan's opening 'Today we got up, got in the mini-bus, and went to . . .'

The speakers assume an audience for whom the day's events have to be made both syntactically and meaningfully more explicit as they would not have to do in ordinary conversation.

Alan initiates the recording and very quickly gets into difficulties; he stutters and, using the style appropriate to a broadcast handover quite confidently, calls in Karen to help him.

Karen is much more able to sustain this audience-directed oral style; her sentences are extended and contain asides like the reference to the terrible stink in the horsebox. She rounds off her opening with a signal to the audience – 'and this is how we were' – and the change of tense that follows signals an attempt to recreate something like a live commentary.

Karen: Well, as we were walking down the – um – pigpen, pigpens, inside where they weighed the pigs, there was one, and – um it was a really big fat one, it had just been weighed. And it had all fleas on its nose and you could see it, it was really terrible, the smell, and all the fleas were hopping about, and he wasn't worrying, he was just going snort snort. And um – they weighed this great big pig, and it was half a hundred weight. That's what Ifor said, because he said they're usually about half a hundred weight. He was ever so big. Over to Alan.

Karen made a transcript of her recording when she went back to school after the field week and some of the differences between this and the oral version suggest that she has developed a consciousness of different spoken and written models.

1a. *From Karen's subsequent written version of her recording*

Well, um, at the Cattle Market, there were lots of calfs. And the calfs were making more noise than their Mothers, and Fathers. And all the other animals pens we went past we heard bah, bah or moo and then we all had a conversation with them so they said, 'bah', and we said 'bah' then a cow said 'moo'. So we said 'Moo' and all the men the um sellers were all wondering what on earth we were all on about. And then suddenly this horse box came along and you could tell that there were lots of pigs in there because the smell was really terrible, and this man came out of the driving seat and he had this great long walking stick you see and he was hitting all of the pigs on their hides, and the pigs must of had ever so hard skin because they were just walking along you know as pigs do. Well when we were walking along side the pig pens. Well we saw where they weighed the pigs, and – um – there was one there and he was half of a hundred weight and he had lots of fleas climbing about every where and he was simply covered in mud thick brown mud.

She elaborates her oral language in a number of ways in transcription. Sentence structures are elaborated; compare the second sentence of Karen's talk with that from the transcript:

'And all the other animals pens we went past we heard bah, bah or moo and then we all had a conversation with them so they said, "bah", and we said "bah" then a cow said "moo" so we said "Moo" . . .'

She has a tendency to formalize her vocabulary to something more appropriate to a written register – 'all these men' become 'sellers'. She also omits phrases which may possibly seem inappropriate to her written style; the reference to the terrible stink does not appear in her transcript.

Her comments on the pig with fleas on his nose is made in the transcript into an ordered sentence:

> 'there was one there and he was half of a hundred weight and he had lots of fleas climbing about every where and he was simply covered in mud, thick brown mud . . .'

The oral version is more jumbled and also more vivid, a succession of sense impressions; the use of the past continuous tense also helping to recreate the actuality of the event.

Karen also adds certain oral tags to her transcript;

Oral: he had this great big walking stick and . . .
Transcr: he had this great long walking stick you see

and

Oral: they were just waddling along not worrying . . .
Transcr: they were just walking along as pigs do

These tags, 'you see', 'as pigs do', etc., seem to make the language more like that of a good children's story; they are more orientated towards a reader.

2. The Pet Shop: Karen

Karen: And – um – I went into the small pet shop and before I went in I tried to read this sign and it went Abergagoobabarggoo pet-shop and, um, eh, then I went in and I saw these lovely cocker spaniels and they were really lovely. They must have been only about three weeks old and I went up to the man, and I said, 'excuse me could you tell me how much these little cocker spaniels are, because I like them everso much.' So he came up to me and he said: 'Well, me love, one pound, two pound, four pound, six pound, take you pick, anything from one pound, to six pound.' So I knelt down and I looked in these little bars, and they were all yapping their heads off, and, um, I was stroking them, and he said, 'Which one do you want?' and I said, 'Oh, I don't want to buy one I was just looking at them', and before I could finish he went, 'Oh, I don't want to bother with you, I got other people to think of', he said, 'how about all the people that want to buy things, I don't want to bother with people that just want to know the prices.' So we went out . . . and then we went on to the jewellery counter and there was this man from Pakistan, and they had these lovely carvings of um, deers, hand-carved, and they were really lovely, for about eight and six.

2a. From Karen's subsequent written version of the same episode

Well when we had all finished in the Cattle Market we all walked past the saddlers shop and – um – there was everything you could think of for a horse. There was saddles, bridles, horse shoes, riding hats, riding boots and even the special little brush for a horse, then we went on to the other market where they sold jewellery, fruit, anything that would be useful for the house or yourself. And – um – I went to the small pet shop and – um – before I went in I tried to read the sign and it said 'ccecadoabergagenceynorackovajkmpeeopne' Pet Shop and – um – then I went in and I saw these tiny cockcrspaniels and they were really lovely. They must have been only three weeks old and so I went up to the Man and said 'Excuse me could you tell me how much these little dogs are' and he replied (in a Welsh accent) 'One, two, three, four, six pound, take your pick which one do you want' so I said 'Oh I don't want to buy one I just wanted to know', and as soon as I could finish he went mad, you know. He was everso kind when he thought I was going to buy one and after that he just didn't want to know me.

Wouldn't it be true to say that Karen's transcript of her visit to the Pet Shop loses much of the liveliness of the oral originals? Conversations seem to be quite authentic in her telling:

'Excuse me, could you tell me how much these little cocker-spaniels are, because I like them ever so much . . .'
becomes:
'Excuse me could you tell how much these little dogs are'.

3. Two Boys in Search of a Language: John and Robin

John and Robin are in an unstreamed second-year class in a mixed urban comprehensive school.* Most of the children in the school, including these two boys, come from working class families.

On this occasion, the teacher had asked the boys to read and discuss two poems and to record their discussion.

Robin begins, and his first words indicate that he sees the task as 'making a tape', like making a radio programme. The tape-recorder is not to be merely a neutral monitor of a natural conversation. Instead, a potential audience is held in mind and Robin speaks to it as well as to John,

Robin: This is John — and Robin — discussing two poems from the book *Voices*. The first one is going to be read by me, Robin —, on p102, poem 94, called 'Girl, Boy, Flower, Bicycle' by M. K. Joseph.
[*Reads the poem:*]
This girl
Waits at the corner for
This boy
Freewheeling on his bicycle.
She holds
A flower in her hand
A gold flower
In her hand she holds
The sun
With power between his thighs
The boy
Comes smiling to her
He rides

* v. also Seven Situations 5: The Aryans page 44.

A bicycle that glitters like
The wind.
This boy this girl
They walk
In step with the wind
Arm in arm
They climb the level street
To where
Laid on the glittering handlebars
The flower
Is round and shining as
The sun.

John begins the discussion. He too has a clear idea of the format that is called for.

John: Robin, I am here to interview you about the poem you have just read. What do you think of it?

The language is formal: *I am*, *you have*; not *I'm*, *you've*. The game is interviews. Robin plays along.

Robin: I think it is very good.

He signals his acceptance of the interviewee role in at least four ways: (1) He repeats the main word of the question (*think*), a feature of formal language (in informal language he would be likely to say simply *it's very good*); (2) he uses *think*, not the word which is used in informal situation in his language – *reckon* (see lines later); (3) he says *it is*, not *it's*; (4) he produces a total, simple definite judgement – *it is good*.

The language they are using isn't in fact the language of interviews as we hear it on television, but their own stereotype of such a language. Actual interviews have *I'm*, *you've*, *it's*. These boys seem to be speaking formal *written* language.

Robin now punctures the atmosphere of formality by the irreverence, in this context, of a statement which belongs to the everyday universe of discourse of the twelve-year old.

Robin: I think it is very good. I wish I had a bike like that kid's

John: How do you know what bike it is ? It might have
             been an old boneshaker.
Robin: [*Laughs.*] It was probably a new Chopper.
John: [*Very fast and low, as if it's unimportant but must be
             said before he can move on.*] But this poem is very
             old.

John as interviewer affects to take Robin's point seriously and at the
same time enters into the spirit of Robin's irreverence with *old bone-
shaker*. But he wants to get back to his formal interview, and the last
remark is there as a transition. He goes on in a normal voice.

John: But on the whole, what did you think the poem
             was about ?
Robin: I think it was about some boy who meets a girl and
             trying to pick her up. And she was showing him
             . . . showing him a flower to show off.
John: But it seemed to me that the girl knew the boy and
             the boy was going to meet her there. That's what it
             says.
Robin: Does it ?
John: If you read the first three lines.
Robin: Oh yes. She was waiting for him.
John: Well, what did you think of the poem ?
Robin: Oh, I reckon it was good.
John: Well, why did you think it was good ?
Robin: Cause, cause it was, cause it involved only a few
             people.
John: Is that all you think was good about it ? Don't you
             think it was interesting the way they were going
             about ?
Robin: Yes, it was, and the way it said, like, 'They climbed
             the level streets'.
John: What, did you get some ideas what the place was
             like ?
Robin: Yes, like not many cars in it, it's a long road and
             you know lots of houses on the side and not many
             [? people's] playing out.

John: What time of the night or morning do you think it was?

Robin: I reckon it was about one o'clock.

John: At what?

Robin: In the afternoon.

John: Thank you, Robin.

As an attempt to get to grips with a poem this is very poor. What is interesting about it to me is the difference between the language of the two boys. After his first answer, *I think it is very good*, everything Robin says is in the sort of language he would normally use talking to a friend. Either he feels a fool playing at interview language or he can't use it, isn't good enough at it to be able to say real things in it; and after all, what he has to say is fairly intractable because he isn't clear about it. John's language on the other hand is not entirely that of informal talk between friends but retains suggestions of a formal public situation. (Part of the basis of this impression is the intonation, which I haven't attempted to set down.) Admittedly it is easier to ask questions in a formal language than to answer them, but it seems to me that less of a gap is felt by John between formal and informal in his language than by Robin in his. When John says 'But it seemed to me that the girl knew the boy and the boy was going to meet her there,' this has an element of formality (particularly the phrase *it seemed to me* and the presence of *that*), so that it feels to be of a piece with the interview language which has gone before, yet it also serves to carry a real meaning for him. John can get away with being more formal than Robin can with it still sounding like him talking.

Why did Robin select (though he soon goes off it) and John take up and persist with the 'public performance' mode of talking to each other? I think because the activity they were undertaking (reading aloud and discussing a poem) is not one that in their world is undertaken in informal peer-group situations. Everyday language provided no patterns and procedures for such an enterprise, no well-worn rails such as are laid down for gossip, narration of personal experience, discussing news, etc. The interview provided a form which would at least keep them going at points where they had no sense of anything urgently needing to be said. For Robin, who would perhaps feel awkward just sitting down and starting to talk about a poem, the fiction of a public situation requiring an announcement served to break the ice. But as soon as he feels he has something he *wants* to say about the poem, the public form is a hindrance. John on the other hand may be able to make the public form serve his own purposes more effectively.

How can they get away with talking formally when there are just the two of them there, good mates and twelve years old? Well, in a way they *don't* get away with it. Robin has to expose the absurdity of the situation with a humorous remark before he has gone on long and made a fool of himself in his own eyes. John is able to carry on without feeling stupid partly because he has joined in Robin's mockery, partly because the public situation is such a transparent fiction that he couldn't possibly be taken as being serious, and partly because, despite the other two factors, he manages to some extent to assimilate the formal language to his own natural voice. The narrow line between playing at public language and speaking it *in propria persona* is something we will return to.

John goes on – less formal now (notice the second word).

John: Now I'm going to read a poem called 'A Poisonous Tree' by William Blake on page 86, poem number 69.

[The poem is actually *A Poison Tree* and John is a very inaccurate reader. The main text below is what he says; at the right what Blake wrote when that differs.]

John:

I was angry with my friend
I told my wrath, my wrath did end.
I was angry with my foe,
I told it not, my wrath did grow.

And I water it in fears	*water'd*
Day and night with more – my tears	*Night and morning with my tears*
And I sun . . . sinned it with smiles	*sunned*
And soft delightful wiles	*And with soft deceitful wiles*

I grew both day and night	*And it grew*
Till bore and apple bright	*Till it bore an*
And my foe behind it shine	*Beheld*
And I knew that it was mine	*he knew*

Into my garden stole	*And into my garden*
When the night had veiled the pole	

> In the morning glad I see
> My foe outstretched beneath the tree.

Robin, keeping to the same pattern as before, embarks on an interview.

Robin: What do you think of that poem?

But this time John isn't playing.

John: Don't really understand it.

That is the end of the interview. Here without any interruptions is the rest of the tape.

Robin: No [*? nor do I*] but I understand a bit of it.
John: You're not supposed to, I'm not sup ... you're not supposed to understand, you're not supposed to, supposed to understand it, you simply, *do* you understand it.
Robin: Well er you know, this apple, this is
John: Aw, blow you for a lark, you said you know how to do it.
Robin: Oh look, this apple, apple is er, is his foe. You know his, you know
John: No, I don't know.
Robin: [*? Hang on a minute.*] Er, his wrath. It's his wrath. When he keeps
John: Yes all right then, clever boy, what's his wrath? There you are – big word.
Robin: It's his enemy, it's his
John: There you are
Robin: apple. Oh! [*Laughs.*]
John: See, you're the one who knew everything. You said, 'Oh, Mr Medway, I know it all ... [*inaudible*]'.
Robin: Shut up.
John: No.
Robin: No, but you know it's he's wrath. It's his anger.
John: Yes.

Robin:	And he, he don't want to speak it out, like.
John:	Oh, I know what it means now.
Robin:	You know, it's
John:	The wrath's his anger and he don't want to say it to the kid that he really hates, he wants to smash his face in.
Robin:	Yes
John:	He's really got it inside him. It's all bubbling up.
Robin:	Yes.
John:	And then, he waters it to make it grow and grow – well, not really waters it. He feels that it's growing, it's growing, it's growing, until he sees his foe and kills him.
Robin:	Yes
John:	And then he loses all his wrath doesn't he. He don't get angry any more.

Out of what unpromising situations can learning come. John, having made such a hash of reading the poem you would think he could never make sense of it, frustrated perhaps by the difficulty he has had reading and understanding it, vents his disillusionment on the whole proceedings. Robin persists. Then John gets it and expresses his getting it in a rush of excited vigorous language. So in the space of a short transcript we see him move from 'oral work' type of talk to the real talk which is one of the forms of real learning.

Having 'got it', they switch off the tape-recorder. What would they gain, for their purposes, by going back to the poem now? (Another time? Maybe.)

4. One Boy in Search of Himself: Keith

This fifteen-year-old student was taking the CSE examination in English in a few weeks' time. Part of this examination is a test in oral English. The students were asked to form groups of five or six – generally they chose friends, but not exclusively; each student had to give a prepared talk of three to five minutes long; he was allowed to use notes, but not to read a fully prepared statement; there followed a group discussion. Students were judged on their own talk, and on the amount and quality of their contribution to the subsequent discussions.

Keith was one of a group of students who had volunteered to visit a BBC recording studio, and be recorded in a variety of talking situations. They enjoyed discussions in class, were flattered to be accepted for such an outing, and saw it as an opportunity for a trial-run for the examination. The situation in the studio was certainly more formal than their own classroom, but I think it would be true to say that there was no more sense of 'occasion' than is normally present during an examination; moreover, by the beginning of this tape, they had already been discussing other topics with their teacher for twenty minutes – they had warmed up and were relaxed.

Keith is giving a talk. Unlike his peers, he chose not to talk about a hobby, or a controversial topic of current concern. His talk, entitled 'Parents and Teachers', is more personal. It is both 'expressive' and 'speculatory' – loosely, an exploration of two kinds of pressure he felt subjected to: the pressure of parents (and, I suppose, society at large) that he should settle on a career, and his rejection by almost all his teachers. I suppose it would be fair to say that he feels that both parents and teachers have rejected him – that his parents don't want him to do what he wants, *be* what he wants; that his teachers have already decided he is no good (don't want him in a school group going to Norway, would be pleased if he had blotted his copybook in the only subject in which he tries). But I think it would also be fair to state, as a matter of *fact* (not, as this stage, as a matter of *criticism*) that he doesn't make this connection between parents and teachers explicit in his talk. He is at the stage of moving from simply recording his personal experience (relationships, encounters that he *felt* strongly about) towards speculating, generalizing about them – seeing the links between himself and other boys, between the way parents behave and teachers behave. He is not yet capable of removing himself emotionally far enough to be able to make global generalizations. He is perhaps not trying to do so, but he is also not quite capable of doing so consistently. His talk *is* speculatory, but also strongly expressive.

What interests us is that the surroundings were comparatively formal; the situation required Keith to make a sustained utterance with minimal hesitation and no interruption, and to give a talk that clearly had a theme, had a shape, and would provoke interest and subsequent discussion. As we have said earlier, one doubts whether he has ever had to fulfil quite such a task ever before. He doesn't, however, attempt a formal mode of discourse – his vocabulary, syntax, hesitations and false starts all reflect the particular quality of his everyday speech. He is relaxed enough to be making a bid for serious attention without ostensibly signalling in his language 'this is serious'. In a sense he seems to be playing an adult role, undertaking an adult task, on his own terms; it's almost as if he were saying 'I'm *not* an adult; I can't pretend to be one; but I take myself and my problems seriously and you should listen to what I am saying, *not* how I am saying it'. It is almost as if, like John and Robin in the previous transcript, his discovery of himself, what he really wants to say, has allowed him to speak confidently in his own voice and reject role-playing all together.

Keith has been talking for about a minute on the theme of Parents and their ideas about suitable careers for their children.

Keith: You know, most parents, that's what they want you to do – settle down straight away. They don't want you to . . . adventure further than what they did. They had a set um – amount of time, how long they could have to themselves, and that was it. But I want to have longer to meself, and I want to enjoy meself. I don't want to go to work and – do something I don't want to enjoy. If I go to work I want to enjoy what I'm doing. Er – That's what I'd like to do, when I leave school. And the trouble with most parents, they just want you to settle down straight away. But um – er – the – they don't like to accept it – that you're going to adventure further than what they did. And they don't accept it that you're growing up and you want to see more things than what they saw, and

you want to do more things than what they did.
Because, when they were teenagers, the war was
on – the war was on and I think the war has
brought fear into their lives and fear of going
further than what you should, doing things that
they haven't done. But, I think that's what the
war's done to a lot of them – it's brought fear into
them, into their lives.

Um – some – well, some parents I suppose are
too easy with you. They don't – they just let you
do anything. They let you go to school when you
want, and I suppose that's a bad thing, I don't
suppose you should be too easy. But then, you
shouldn't be too formal, we should be more
casual about it – I think most parents should. A
lot of boys can just stay away when they want from
school. And that's when – I suppose, you know,
they start becoming delinquents, and they do
what they want. I don't think you should do that.
And, that's when – and then the teachers realize
that, and then they just accept you as a delinquent.
Whereas, a lot of teachers – er – they just ac – they
just like you or not. They – that's the trouble with
some teachers. If – if you do something wrong in
one subject, then they – and it's not their subject,
then they think, oh well, he done bad in that subject – so – I'll say that he's doing bad in mine,
before they've even listened to you. That's what
happens to me. I'm not feeling sorry for meself or
that, but, you know, if I did try, and then I don't
think I could do any good, because a lot of
teachers, just listen to the staff-room chat, and
they go by that. They've heard what I am. Because, before I come to school, my brothers was
here, and they wasn't all that good, they used to
muck about. And I was accepted as bad, when I
came, although I am, but if I wasn't – if I intended
to really try, I thi – you know, I don't think I

would have been able to get on, because some teachers just wouldn't have accepted it, that I was going to try, because me brothers were there and so – they wouldn't accept it that I would. And – this is the trouble with a lot of teachers, and now that – um – I'm not all that bright or I muck about quite a lot, they just – they just got the same against me, they you know, even if I try now. That – that's their lot. You know – I've just got no chance. And the other day. 'Teacher', I said to the teacher, 'Um, Sir, when will we be going to Norway, because I'm interested in it,' so he said: 'Well, we've been picking it out of an hat, because there's so many who want to go,' he said 'I'm sure your name will come out.' Because he said 'I don't want you to go really,' and I'm sure if they picked it out of an hat my name would come out cos I don't think they do it fairly anyway, and so that's what I reckoned 'ld happen to me, and some boys who haven't done anything wrong. They – they just get accepted as something different to what they are. If they've done one thing bad, then everything's supposed to be bad to them.

But some teachers are all right. They accept you as you are in that period, whether, you know, that's what they should do, but others just accept you as something else. They think that you're bad and you'll always do bad. Just like this morning when I got called out of lessons, cos the teacher wanted to see me. The – teacher – when I came back the teacher said 'I see that's all you are a scholar of English', he thought I got the cane or something, and so – he – cos he wanted me to get the cane, off this teacher. He wanted me to have done something bad cos he – that's the only sub- ject I try in and he knows it, and so when – when I told him 'No you're wrong sir', he just went all red and was right choked and said 'don't be in-

solent', and that's what mainly – most of the
teachers do to me because I'm marked I suppose,
and that's what happens to a lot of boys.

5. Discussion of Keith's Talk

Keith's friends then proceed to discuss his talk. The first thing
that one notices is that the discussion centres not on the final section of Keith's talk but on the less personal matter of jobs and
careers. Perhaps his peers have heard Keith's story before, and
take it all with a pinch of salt; perhaps the slightly formal situation
of a BBC studio precludes the expression of sympathy, and the
frank appraisal of the truth of Keith's complaint.

But it is a real discussion – an exploration together. Keith's
peers are weighing the validity of what he has said. Some of what
he says strikes Brian as unreasonable. He does reject Keith's attitude, but not I think out of hand – he is trying to persuade Keith,
and understand him.

Brian: Well what I thought – what I thought you said
         about – er – parents not wanting you to venture
         out, and soon as you leave school get a job and
         settle down and get security an' that. I think if – if
         you go to a grammar school that – that is – what
         you've really got to do. I mean, you leave school
         when you're sixteen, nearly seventeen and – and
         you apprenticeship, maximum age in most jobs,
         is what, seventeen isn't it, so that means as soon
         as you leave you – you've got to get an apprentice-
         ship, if you're not, you know, all that bright
         academically, you wanna sort of go willing in one
         thing, you – you've got to get an apprenticeship.
Keith: Oh but that's entirely different because that is
         something – but if you want to do it, you will do it.
         You won't be made to do it because you know that
         if you want that job you've got to do it, but whereas
         some other people, they might – they might not
         want to go to work straight away, well I don't. I

don't want just to work straight away, and that's that, and just settle down for the rest of my life, I just don't want to do that, I mean –

Stan also rejects Keith's proposition; but first he tries to define his attitude. Later he tries to point out the danger of relying on the fact that he has had a grammar school education – will this be so valuable an entrée to jobs in ten years time?; and would he feel as confident if he were attending a secondary (modern) school? He is trying to test the validity of Keith's attitude and get Keith himself to see all round the problem.

Stan: You're living for the present and not for the future. You know, you're not thinking about –

Keith: No, I'm not worried about oh I'll go to this job, cos when I'm sixty-five I'll get a good pension and that'll be very good for me, cos I – I don't want to think about that.

Alan supports Stan's first statement and takes it further: OK, we'll accept for the moment that you don't need to settle down straight away; when will you settle down? Let's get your proposition clear, and its implications.

Alan: Well you've got to sometime though. You've got to think about it sometime, when will you start thinking about it?

Keith: Yeah, but if I'm sixteen I'm not going to start thinking about when I'm seventy-five.

Alan: That's what I'm saying, when will you start thinking about it?

Keith: When I'm seventy-five

Alan: Thinking about a job?

Keith: NO, I – I start to think about a pension. I mean I'll think about a job when I'm about twenty-five, really – to settle down – I don't want to settle down till then –
[*Talking together.*]

Keith: Not really, what's late then? How old would you say is late to settle down?

Alan:	What do you mean settle down – like with a family or with a job?
Keith:	No, settle down in a job. The same job every day – just doing the same thing every day.
Alan:	Well I think round the twenty mark.
Keith:	Well, how about twenty-five, is that too late?
Alan:	I think it is a bit too late.
Brian:	I think the best idea is for – what you get in many of the secondary schools, when they leave fifteen, they leave and then – then – they haven't – they haven't, they've no qualifications and – that's why you get – a lot of your mates, you say, 'You've left, you've left – er – school then, what d'you work as?' and they go 'Gor' – they go – 'I've had about fifteen jobs since I left school' and that's how it is, they're trying to do what you're trying to do. They're – they're doing every type of job that they can find possible, to find the one that really suits them, the one they can enjoy and settle down in . . .
Keith:	Well if they're going to stick to that one job for the rest of their life, then it is, surely, it's worth doing that?
Brian:	That's what, that's what I mean, I – tha – they've tried all the jobs and that's the one that they like the best and if – if you feel the way they did, wouldn't it have been better for you to leave when you was – er – fifteen?
Keith:	Well I still am
Brian:	Well at Easter when you could have left Summer?
Keith:	I – I don't want to do that, because I'll always have a grammar school education, I – you know – at least I've got that behind me if I leave when I – I'll still be fifteen when I leave, but I'll still have that behind me when I leave, and I don't want to settle down straightaway, that's all. I want to enjoy myself while I can.
Stan:	But at twenty-five nearly all the schools'll be

	comprehensive and the sort of grammar school education 'll be at the back of people's minds, you know. They won't take it into account so much, I don't think . . . twenty-five and try and get a job.
Keith:	Well maybe that's right, but although you say that, I mean I could just say that about anything. I mean if you leave a year later – if you leave a year later, you still have the grammar school education. Supposing you stay at the same school for say ten years then you leave and then you find out it's too late for me – that's no good – so it's just the same really, but I want to – I don't want to really settle down till I'm about twenty-five, maybe twenty-five, I don't know, but I just don't want to settle – maybe I'll just – just have a year off school and then – then maybe I'll want to settle down, but what I feel now –
Stan:	You're not worried about a job cos you've got – em – you think you've got a grammar school education to get you through it –
Keith:	No.
Stan:	If you went – um – say a secondary school, you know it wasn't much of a school and you left would you be thinking about a job then? You know –
Keith:	No [*talking together*] I'd think about bettering myself really I suppose, because I'd try and venture further and try and earn money different, without you actually having to go to a grammar school, that's what I want to do. I'd like to have a business or something, and travel. I'd like to travel round the world and see more things, and then you know enjoy yourself that way.
Brian:	I think most – most – I don't know whether it's true of you – most pe – most parents of people that go to grammar school they think 'Ah my little Jimmy, you know, he's a nice little boy really and he's going to get a nice job, and settle down,' but

really, you know, the – the kid, he doesn't want to, so in his mind he thinks 'Oh I'll do what they say', but in his subconscious mind he thinks 'I'll go against them. I don't want to do as they say', and he gets all frustrated and the sort of parents try to sort of own the boy, you know what I mean.

None of them accepts what Keith has to say but they try to get him to clarify, expand, perceive the problems. They are themselves witholding final decisions, they are speculating, encouraging Keith to speculate, keeping the ball in the air. They are working together, but also *with* Keith. It is a discussion not a concerted attack, not even an argument – its tone allows Brian (at his second utterance) to support Keith (sometimes some boys positively benefit from not settling down straight away).

In part this is a social act: 'We have been asked to try to discuss this topic for five minutes, let's discuss it reasonably; if we are too categorical the discussion will stop or end in violent disagreement.' They are behaving sociably.

In part it is an intellectual act. They know, they have come to realize, that there are no right answers, that the search for truth demands that one inhibits spontaneous acceptance or rejection of an idea, that one explores it tentatively, nudging away at it and one's opponent in an attempt to find the chinks. But not, I think, the chinks in Keith's armour, rather the chinks in his, and their own arguments. The tone and pace are relaxed; there is no irritation, they are not trying to score, they are trying to get at the truth. It is only the beginning of the discussion, they don't get very far in this excerpt, but they are approaching the problem and the discussion situation in the right way. At the very simplest level, they listen to one another; they give each other time to express themselves, develop a point; they rarely interrupt.

Of course, there are hesitations, false starts, clumsy constructions. Brian's first remarks, for instance, could be put more briskly and with more immediate clarity: 'But wouldn't it be true to say that if you leave school at sixteen you really can't afford to play around for long? Someone like us needs further qualifications if he is to get on. You'll get these qualifications by taking up an apprenticeship, and you have to do this before you are seventeen, in most trades.' But even an adept conversationalist is unlikely to speak as accurately and clearly as he writes; and if he did mightn't he, by his very efficiency, kill conversation stone dead? Our hesitancies are, once again, both social and rational. They indicate our uncertainty, our humility – 'I am not an all-conquering ogre, you can safely join issue with me' – ; they invite speculation. They also indicate we ourselves are still speculating.

It is of course a question of degree. I would conjecture that, with more practice, these boys would become less clumsy; but I would hope that they would never lose their tentativeness.

When we are participating in a discussion we are not fundamentally concerned to consider how good it is – though we might well refuse to participate because for one reason or another we feel that the discussion is profitless. But teachers, and parents (and of course, increasingly, examiners) may well be interested to consider this question; and the value of such a discussion to the participants. Do we, as parents, approve of the fact that part of the school day is being spent in this way? Do we, as teachers, consider these particular students have learnt, are learning anything? The problem is complicated: as suggested elsewhere in the book, are teachers able to value the skills their children already possess? do they try to develop other skills that may not necessarily be of any more value?

Tentatively I would suggest that, here, under the pressure of the formal situation, these students are formulating, testing and revising their view of the world. They are confirming or enlarging each other's understanding of some of the basic facts of living. They are getting practice and confidence with words. They are indulging in a social and rational act. They are helping each other to behave graciously and to think rationally.

If our pupils are to develop these qualities and skills, they need practice – sometimes, I suggest, in the presence of teacher-adults who can guide, restrain, encourage; sometimes alone with a small group of their peers, free of the inhibitions created by the presence of an adult and an audience thirty strong, free to explore, to make mistakes.

Of course, they also need more experience to draw upon. Discussion without a basis of experience would very quickly become trivial and pointless. The teacher can help to provide further inputs of such experience (every subject in the school curriculum offers the pupil its own quota of data). But if the experience is to be valuable it must be digested. We digest new experience by talking about it with ourselves, with our peers, with our elders. In this discussion they are with their peers, but traces of previous solitary musing, and of guidance by their teachers, are visible too. Such discussion is fundamental to their growth.

Like Keith, all the participants, are in part playing a role – pretending for the moment to be serious adults engaged in the sort of discussion they will have seen on television, but rarely participate in in playground or classroom. But the role has become one that they can convincingly act – they are not embarrassed, nor do they fool around.

6. Progress in Talk

In the preceding sections we have been concerned to illustrate talk in a variety of situations. We feel that a question many teachers would be concerned to ask is: Is there such a thing as progress in talk skills? And, what naturally follows: Can parent and teacher promote progress, and by what means? Does the curriculum and organization of a particular school *help* those who are so concerned?

We could have explored such a topic by asking one of our group to construct a personal statement. We felt, however, that it might, in this book, be of some interest to present our readers with a complete transcript of our group's discussion. We suggest that, if you are simply interested in any conclusions we reached, you should turn to the end of this section for a resumé of the points we made. You may, however, also be interested to consider two things: do these adults – who are after all fairly experienced in peer-group discussions (the present book is the fruit of many months such discussion) – display any mastery of talk superior to that displayed by the many children whose talk is transcribed earlier in the book? Is the mastery, if it exists, total – are these adults 'better' in every way than the children; can they go further themselves? Are there kinds of talk not displayed here, kinds that are important? In what way is mastery of any talk skills important?

You might also be interested to consider our attempt to chart our own discussion, by examining the headings and comments inserted in the transcript.* What we have tried to do is to notice how our talk moved from tentative, slightly random, stabs at our topic, on to first formulations – 'is this, then, what we are say-

* The headings in small roman type offer a running *précis* of the discussion; those in italics attempt to indicate our discussion 'strategies'

ing?'; sometimes into illustrations drawn from our own experiences that confirm our hypotheses; then back again to further stabs. Is this, in itself, a mode of exploration through talk that can lead to the best results? Is it a mode that can only occur naturally among peers who know each other well, and feel relaxed enough to try out an idea and let it go easily if it is seen to be inadequate?

Our discussion is not of course in any way complete. We didn't consider, among other things, talk that is used as a screen to hide behind, or as a device to deceive or manipulate others; we only touched on the skills of the raconteur. And it may, like all transcripts, strain the patience of all but the most committed reader. We did consider cutting it, isolating the most 'interesting' things, and reducing the hesitancies, repetitions, false starts, syntactical 'errors' that characterize talk. We have certainly been embarrassed to be faced in print with remarks and attitudes that, in the flow of talk, we hardly noticed. But we haven't changed anything. Our book is about talk; talk is like this, it is not like writing. If we are to study talk we must look at the real thing, not transcripts that have been 'cleaned up' for the printed page. We also felt that the transcript as it stands helps to illustrate some of the things we have come to believe over the months of working on the book. In one sense, 'Talk' is inefficient: when one person is writing a statement he can pause, reconsider, reshape, refine his idea, get it exact; he can chase an elusive thought and pin it down (in talk, an idea may appear momentarily and disappear, perhaps to be lost forever, because no one else picks it up, or something or someone else suddenly dominates the scene). Good talk, too, requires a very special kind of situation – the atmosphere, the relationships, must be right before we can be totally frank with ourselves and each other; and there must be a willingness to listen, to help others in their formulations, not to dominate the scene. On the other hand we do feel that good talk may also help to keep the topic wide open, prevent too early formulations, promote deeper penetration.

Of course no one discussion can totally cover a topic. And, even at the end of an hour and a half, each participant may well feel less than totally committed to any conclusions 'reached'. I suspect that generally no one does feel as committed to something he has 'merely' said. A spoken statement is less likely than a written one to present a final view. On the other hand there is a fair chance that the presence, the contributions, the disagreements of others may help each speaker reach a more total view. We are not, of course, claiming that despite its limitations talk is better than writing; simply that it too has its place, and perhaps that more room should be made for it in our schools.

This brings us to the second reservation we had. We are all teachers – we have a particular kind of interest in talk and its place in the school day; our illustrations are often drawn from our teaching experience. We may, therefore, have put stress on certain aspects of our topic, and undervalued, underexplored others. The very question we are asking is perhaps essentially a teacher's question – a teacher interested in his children, and perhaps eager to explain and justify his teaching-style to head-teacher and parents: is there such a thing as progress in talk, and can it be promoted?

What we have said – 'Good talk . . . requires a very special kind of situation' – is particularly relevant here. It is clear from the transcripts that form the body of the book that some of the children display (at any rate in the talk situations transcribed) more apparent confidence, fluency and command of language – willingness and ability to communicate their ideas and feelings – than do others. In this last chapter we try to define for ourselves what we mean by good talk, and to consider what situations promote this. As teachers we are particularly concerned with this latter question. Most of our readers are likely to agree that teachers, with the best intentions, can only too easily inhibit talk, and with it the opportunity for the child to develop his understanding of the topic in hand, and to formulate for himself his own view of the world and of himself. Our own preference for the kind of 'teaching' illustrated in the Geography Field Trip and the group discussion of the Yevtushenko poem *without* a teacher present, has been clearly indicated in the text, and we hope justified.

We would not however want to suggest that a teacher (or any adult) is the only likely inhibiting factor. Many children, many adults for that matter, are afraid of the reactions of their peer group. Laughter, contempt, disregard, silence, even simple disagreement expressed with quiet confidence effectively discourage the timid from further participation in peer-group talk. We have touched on this problem in the section entitled 'Roles and Models'. One might, here, want to conjecture, for instance, how much harm the young Karen might be doing her own peers by her superlative confidence and only too apparent skill; how, perhaps, Robin's only defence against John during their discussion is to undercut his seriousness and greater mastery of the formal mode by reverting very quickly to the informal and by, deliberately?, introducing the irrelevant and irreverent: 'I wish I had a bike like that kid's . . . It was probably a new Chopper'. We have already suggested that one of the reasons Keith dares to speak so intimately about himself – his ambitions, and pains – is that he feels safe; he knows that his peers will treat him with respect and gentleness. We are convinced that this is not 'natural' – that is, we cannot take it for granted that in time *all* children, without guidance, become such agreeable adolescents and future adults. Such 'progress' depends upon the talk situations we encounter as we grow. Some of us are lucky. As teachers, and parents, we have to try to ensure that the children in our care are given the opportunities to grow by providing them with an appropriate environment: one that allows for talk, that provokes every child to talk, that keeps under some restraint the one enemy – aggressiveness – and tries to break the bonds of that other enemy – timidity.

In our conversation that follows we do refer more fully to these problems; we suggest – 'that somebody who is sufficiently relaxed and adequately confident is likely to indulge in better exploratory talk, analytical talk, than somebody who feels tense and insecure'. And this carries with it the implication that if a child is not sufficiently relaxed and adequately confident the teacher and parent have to do all in their power to help the child, and to create in the classroom and the home the environment that makes real conversation possible.

The transcript follows. You will require some patience, particularly at the start: the first few lines may not make much sense referring, as they do, to something said earlier the same evening. But we hope you will persevere.

1. A Conversation on the Subject: Is there Progress in Talk?

Running in:

Paul: What ... you were saying then, at the beginning ... Susan ...

Susan: I was saying that the idea ... that we were talking about literacy and ... how there are better ... there's a kind of literacy that you were talking about, that you could achieve in exams which somehow was fulfilling, so presumably is ... I don't know ... a sophisticated kind, or a better kind than one could achieve in a noisy room. So we all ... we assume that there ... that there is development in writing ... and I just thought that that would be an interesting way of looking at talk ... because certainly, I mean, do we ... do we think that if somebody was to stand in a room which was otherwise silent, and talk, for er, an hour, would that be better talk than ...

Peter: The difference in the two writing situations is simply that, er, in the ideal situation it's given more attention ... you know, it's concentrated on, whereas in the noisy room it's, you know, thought gets interrupted and er ...

Susan: And is that the same about talk, that when it's concentrated on, by the talkers, even though, perhaps a silly example to say one person, that the way we're concentrating on it now, trying to be precise, well is that better talk than, erm, talk which we don't even realize that we're particularly saying anything?

We begin to focus:

Joan: I think it's different ... I think it's difficult to say that it's better ... it's ... I mean, what is the optimum purpose of talk? (Peter: Mm.)

Susan: That's what I would like to know, whether . . .

Paul: This analytical talk (Joan: Yes.) is likely to be, but
            that may be a very cold kind of talk, and therefore
            something that we only engage in on special oc-
            casions, or on specific occasions.

Peter: Do you mean 'cool' as, as non-cold, non-warm ? I
            mean it's non-er – it's neutral isn't it ? With
            respect to feelings. It's not – er –

Joan: I think you can get very warm and excited about
            speculative talk which is what we're perhaps doing
            at the moment.

Paul: Do you think . . . this is one of the things that . . .
            would it be true that fifth-formers, shall we say,
            who do get very warm er have to learn how to con-
            trol their warmth in order to get closer to the truth
            than they can get when they are warm ?

Joan: Yes, and to allow other people room to respond
            and to think for themselves. But I think you can
            still get a kind of warmth in a group with the ex-
            citement of getting nearer (Paul: Yes. Peter:
            Mm.) what they're looking for.

Susan: That's . . . that's the sort of warmth I thought you
            meant rather than sort of all . . .

Joan: Yes, I really did mean that more than what Paul
            said, but . . .

Susan: Is an, er, sort of distanced objectivity towards
            one's own talk then, when one had that, would
            that mean that there had been progress ? Does a
            little child have that ?

A first formulation: progress implies growth of self-awareness.

Paul: I wouldn't think it would be as sustained, in a little
            child.

Peter: I would have thought the little child was con-
            scious of his talk, at the time when he was playing
            with it, when he was, you know, saying the same
            words seventy times, and er, or making absurd

rhymes – at times like that he's . . . when sort of language becomes, his own language becomes opaque to him, he doesn't go straight through it to the meaning.

What sort of awareness does a young child have of his own language?

Erm – I – maybe it's only the very sophisticated person, or the very self-conscious person, because he's in an exposed position, that he's aware of his own analytical talk in the same way.

Paul: How do you find with Lisa, in fact, aged seven?

Susan: Just trying to think. She is, she is of course, conscious of her talk. I mean, she can manipulate . . . she can hear herself talking and stand outside it and see what effects . . . effect it's having, and she already knows about different kinds of appropriateness. She can manage me and other people through the kind of talk she chooses to use, and I suppose that's fairly typical at seven or eight. But she can't hold an abstract idea – and search out new approaches to the idea with other people – as far as I know.

Does progress imply an ability to handle abstract ideas?

But she might do this with groups of children. But I mean I – I would have thought, erm, I haven't really thought very freshly about it; I would have thought *that* would show progress in talk, but of course, not just in talk.

Paul: Yes. My suspicion would be that a child isn't actually very interested in the kind of subject that one subjects to analysis, to analytical talk. That he might be temporarily intrigued by an idea but he's not really so involved.

Susan: No. I mean they might raise the issue as she does about 'infinite' or 'is there a god?', but beyond about ten sentences it's dismissed, (Paul: Mm.)

	and the subject's changed, to something more concrete.
Peter:	Hmm. I mean that raised the question of how far progress in talk is progress in intellect, you know, in the ability to form operations and all that, doesn't it ? (Joan: Yes.) Or growth of logic.

Rounding off the section:

Susan:	And we're assuming that abstract ideas demand a greater sophistication ?
Peter:	And the behaviourists and the systems analysis boys talk about erm, er . . . teaching discussion skills, don't they ? (Joan: Yes.) They say it should be one of the objectives of English teaching – should be discussion skills.

New section: skills.

	Er . . . I wonder if we can get anywhere by thinking about that sort of term ? Whether it is a matter of skills.
Joan:	Well, you admire the Humanities Project (Susan: Yes.), and there is an indication of skills there.

Group discussion.

	(Susan: Yes. Peter: Mm.) You're feeding in new ideas, and bringing people in who haven't contributed much . . .
Susan:	Yes. I think there are definite skills and I think Paul would agree with that. And true our experience with students shows that, er, they do feel that that is so . . . but, of course, it just depends what you mean by skills.
Peter:	You know, this is the problem, isn't it ? Because some people object to skills because it suggests a sort of narrow – er – you know, sort of habit response, and thus use the term to mean anything that can be done skilfully, don't they ? (Group:

175

Mm.) Anything which, you know, behaviour which, while learning ... I mean, it's hard to think of any behaviour which isn't, in a way.

Paul: I think one of the things that I notice with students, and I think the same would be true for Keith and his friends* there, is, erm, that they've got beyond the stage where they have to, as it were, establish themselves, as a personality, therefore they don't have to fight for a position in the group or be so, erm, determined not to have to fight, 'I'm not going to play this game', that they withdraw. So that the problem is to establish that, erm, friendliness,

A social attitude necessary to progress.

and obviously the group do a lot of this themselves at coffee, and outside your control anyhow, but there does come a time after they've been working together for, say, three months, when, erm, the group does begin to coalesce (Peter: Mm.), and there can therefore be pauses for reflection, and a willingness to withhold your immediate thought, in order to try and help the last speaker move a step further, and this is a social skill which they don't in a sense acquire, because they might well have had it with members of their family, but that they can now use with the members of their group, because they and their group have now got to that stage.

Joan: Do you think this goes on, perhaps, to giving them the ability to use it in a number of more public situations,

The wider group.

where they don't even know the group as well as

* v. Section 5/5 page 161.

| | the one in college ? (Paul: Yes.) and is this a progress ... until ... ? |
| Susan: | Yes. And I think that all – all these things, I mean ... er ... when, when we do see that, what we regard as progress with students, I'm never thinking, 'Oh well, now they'll be better teachers, because they'll be able to run discussions in the classroom', |

Personal growth through discussion skill.

> ... I very rarely think that; I think, well they've made a very great leap forward in their everyday lives. Because I know when I managed to acquire some of those skills

Autobiographical example:

> it had a fre ... it shif ... it shifted the way I looked at other people, tremendously. I really began to listen to other people and learn from the people that previously I'd have been blocked off from.

Peter:	Go on – well, when was this, Susan ?
Susan:	When what ?
Peter:	How old were you ?
Susan:	Oh, only about three years ago, so I'd be ...
Peter:	Oh, I see.
Susan:	Well, I mean ... it's strange isn't it ? You can pick up something like that handbook, and for it to change you so radically [*laughing*], when other people do it [*laughing*] through 'Sons and Lovers'. And I really did start to, in discussions quite insincerely, to say to people, 'How interesting', or 'Go on – how old were you ?' I'm not suggesting you were saying it insincerely at all, I know you weren't. But I couldn't, I couldn't have done that about five years ago.

Peter:	And this was the Humanities Project that ... handbook ...
Susan:	Well, it wasn't the whole project ... I just looked through the handbook, and I thought well, this is very true, and this where I've gone ... gone wrong and ... not only as a teacher, but as a person. I haven't ever really listened with genuine interest to anybody except somebody that I, you know, already loved, as it were. But to do it cold, with people who were completely alien to me, I'd never done it in any sort of educational or social situation.
Peter:	Yeah.
Susan:	But maybe I was unusually retarded in that respect ... but I think erm, a lot of people are ...
Peter:	I find with strangers that it's mm ... I find it hard to talk to them at first because I ... I find it hard to concentrate on what they're saying because I'm too concerned with defending myself from (Susan: Mm.) attack or exposure or something

Inhibited by insecurity – *another personal example.*

	(Paul: Mm.) so all the time I'm – er – I see it as a sort of parrying, and I have to counter every move, you know, rather than as a sort of co-operative thing, where you're arriving at a common understanding.
Susan:	Because all the time someone else is speaking you're phrasing and re-phrasing your reply to that person, aren't you? (Peter: Yes.) As well as trying to listen to them. And it's a very complex thing to have to do.
Peter:	And you don't always stand back and trust yourself to your real reaction ... er ... (Susan: No.) ...
Susan:	Or if there is such a thing as 'a real reaction.'
Peter:	It seems like ...
Paul:	Isn't it a snag then that a child, then, or an im-

178

mature person does trust himself, herself, to a 'real' reaction and it can get in the way, because they will burst in, in the middle of a statement

But is some kind of inhibition necessary?

(Group: Mm.), and pick up something comparatively minor (Group: Mm.), and sidetrack therefore, an interesting development (Susan: Mm. Peter: Yes, yes.) in the talk, and possibly also exacerbate feeling by picking up the emotional tone of one word, because they'd misread that word (Susan: Mm.), instead of trying to see the overall intentions of the previous speaker?

Susan: And they're always people, those people, who have – erm – problems of feeling real, or whatever, I would see it as feeling real, like, sort of . . . . . . or somebody like that, one of our students who would be angry at things I hadn't even noticed somebody else had said. (Group: Mm.) You know, he'd be racing off on that, and interrupting.

Joan: Yes, it is a lack of detachment, isn't it? And an ability (Paul: Mm.) not to be able to stand back, and see that opinions don't attack you, even if you don't hold them,

Acceptance of disagreement.

and it goes, I think, with being able to love people with whom you radically disagree (Paul: Mm.), which is again something I think which comes a bit later.

Susan: So if we talk about agreement and disagreement, do we think that it's more sophisticated to be able to discuss erm controversial issues then? I mean if we were now . . . if er say . . . . . . and people who have trouble discussing controversial things, if they were to sit down and to discuss say er . . . I don't know, er . . . a menu – actually I think

	somebody like that would probably turn it into a controversial issue – that seems to me to need a less sophisticated kind of talk than to sit down and to discuss something that's really problematic.
Joan:	To explore, rather than to (Susan: Mm.) argue.
Susan:	Because erm, erm, surely what we're looking for is for people to accept a 'don't know' situation in their talk. (Group: Mm.)

Toleration of uncertainty.

Paul:	I think this goes back to what Joan was saying earlier about being able to use this mode among comparative strangers, once you've actually developed it. I certainly found for many years it was impossible to talk at a LATE meeting because I was frightened

Further personal testimony: growing out of insecurity, attending to others.

	(Peter: Mm.) of the numbers, even when there were only 40, and then I had to chair a session maybe 2 or 3 years ago and I found I had by that stage managed to be sufficiently relaxed not to feel in any sort of danger (Peter: Yes.) such as you've (Peter: Yes.) mentioned, and that I was able therefore to take these statements exactly as I used to take them from kids in class (Peter: Mm.) and not myself react, except to imply, 'That was interesting. (Peter: Mm.) Can somebody come in on that?' (Group: Mm.) So that it was detachment, it was not becoming too emotionally involved to the extent of feeling threatened myself or having to defend (Peter: Yes.), or having to defend my point of view.
Peter:	It's sort of feeling – you have to feel, erm, freedom from strain and risk in order to – give your attention fully to the . . . (Paul: Yes.) I suppose . . . to,

	to what's going on – you have to, erm, I suppose you have to feel you have a sort of secure base in order to er let your attention go outwards.
Joan:	Isn't it also focusing on the exploration, on the talk, rather than on any . . . any . . . personal relationship that (Susan: Mm.) you're having with (Paul: Mm.) people involved in it. (Group: Mm.) I mean, I'm always saying to students when they're nervous on teaching practice,

A supporting example:

	'If you think about whatever material it is you're concerned with, and the children, and not yourself, if you can focus on that, don't – don't think about not thinking about yourself but focus on something that is important, then you – you will find that you are not so nervous.' I mean, if you, I
Rounding off:	. . . if you were in a play, the thing that gets through is that you're focusing on the character and your audience reaction and not on yourself.
Paul:	Then in a sense what we're beginning to suggest is that somebody who is sufficiently relaxed and adequately confident is likely to indulge in better exploratory talk (Peter: Yes.): analytical talk, than somebody who feels tense and insecure.

A new start:

Peter:	Just to er . . . if we're . . . at the stage now of throwing in things very haphazardly . . . erm – one of the criteria of progress in talk might be the sort of range of subject matter that's encompassed by one's talk.

Progress implies: scope of talk;

	(Joan: Yes. Paul: Mm.) In other words, maybe a a good talker is someone who talks about a lot of things. Erm, you know, and talks in a lot of differ-

181

ent situations. There was a bit, there was an article by erm, V. S. Naipaul or somebody in the Listener, and he commented on that he was very impressed by Norman Mailer because Mailer he says has such a very coherent and adaptable sort of philosophy, which is constantly getting up-dated. So that when he goes round and exposes himself to new situations all the time as he does, and something happens to him, he immediately talks about it and fits it in and has – er – has a line on it, develops a line on, by talking about it. Erm, well, this is someone who's putting talk to use for his own purposes; he's keeping his sort of world in one piece ... erm ... and maybe it's this ... it's seeing all areas of experience as talkable about, that is, you know, one of the signs of the good talker.

Paul: I think, you know – I mean I take, I take that point ... I think I feel myself that ... erm ... it's more a question of being able to talk in a multitude of different social contexts, rather than to talk about a variety of different topics in the *same* kind of social context.

Competence in range of social situation.

I mean one could, one could admire somebody who could talk about, shall we say, the American political situation, and Vietnam, and Russia (Peter: Boxing.), and boxing, and education (Peter: Mm.), but all one would be saying there is, 'Such diversity of interest, so wide in his sympathies, where does he find time to experience all these things? Or to read about them? Or to be so informed?' Erm, but he's just clever. But whereas somebody who can talk in a ... s ... in an academic seminar, who can chat up ordinary blokes in the pub, who can – um – get on very well with 5 year olds, in the playgroup or whatever

	(Peter: Mm.), this seems to me to be using a diversity of skills which I think I would be inclined to say is the mark of a better talker.
Susan:	Yes, I think I would agree with that.
Joan:	Because you've also got to be a good listener haven't you? (Paul: Yes.)
Peter:	The problem you come up against all the time is that um – I mean one . . . we all know er some super-talkers. They're – er – ma . . . (Susan: Muggeridge.) . . . master-talkers. Who?
Susan:	People like Muggeridge.
Peter:	Well . . . I was thinking of people I know (Susan: Oh.) . . . that I've been in a lot of situations with, and they've talked in all of them, they've always had something to say. Er – on the other hand one's very thankful that not all one's friends are like that (Paul: Mm.), so, erm, you know, how far is this something we want for everybody?

Does everyone *have* to talk?

	There are . . . I've got some very silent friends, and, you know, one in particular, whose . . . doesn't seem any . . . you know, I don't value him any the less because he's . . . doesn't say very much. And . . . and . . .
Susan:	How . . . how can you know . . .
Peter:	. . . and one feels that he's . . . he's, erm, he's participating in the conversation, he's real, even though he doesn't say anything.
Susan:	Yes, because he probably makes very economic contribution. I couldn't . . . I couldn't love (Peter: Mm.) somebody who was totally silent, I don't think, as a friend (Peter: No.); I'd find that very . . . well, I mean not, I don't just mean totally silent, because nobody is, but I mean, who just use language in a simple transactional way – that would be hard to . . . I mean, that somebody had . . . would have to be reflective for me (Peter:

	Mm, mm.), to be, you know . . . but that could be very economic, because I remember . . .
Peter:	This chap's a painter. (Group: Mm.)
Susan:	Yes – I was going to talk about whether erm having all this kind of talk is a very varied kind of – er – medium, is much like a painter (Peter: Yes.), using a whole variety of – er – techniques with it?
Paul:	I've certainly found art main students . . . er . . . in basic and curriculum English are frequently not so op . . . so capable of talk, er, not so capable of either social talk or analytical talk . . . as if . . .
Joan:	Language isn't their medium, is it? (Paul: No.)

There are other ways . . .

Peter:	What I wonder is whether, you know, it's a bad thing – whether it's a lack that matters? (Paul: Yes.) Or whether it's just a choice? You know, not to operate in that sort of way.
Susan:	Well, how would you judge whether it mattered or not? By something like the way the world was going? Or, er, their personal sort of sanity? Or . . . how . . . how could one tell?

But most people would like to.

Paul:	I certainly (Peter: Mm.) sort of feel inadequate in a number of social situations and wish I didn't. And er, therefore maybe certain basic skills, or skills to cope with certain common situations, might be desirable I think I've heard students say, 'I'm not very good at talking – I wish I were, I feel so shy; I haven't got anything to say.'
Susan:	Well, that's bec . . . what we were talking about before, that, erm, I mean, if one feels constrained to – to say something clever or rather to be silent because one can't say anything clever, there's nothing more . . . deadening to this kind of talk. I mean, I'm not . . . I'm not really . . . I mean, I'm

listening to myself to see if what I say sounds erm interesting to me and is helping to push my ideas forward at this very moment, but I'm not particularly – I don't particularly mind if I say something stupid or unjust, whereas I think a lot of people are very riddled with fear

Talk *can* be a high-risk situation.

(Paul: Yes.) that they'll say something stupid – and people that I know, sometimes, and that I've been only too glad to get out of my acquaintance, have taken every discussion as an opportunity to show how clever they are . . . that's an awful bind (Peter: Of course it is, yes.) isn't it ?

A new section: pleasures of relaxed talk.

Joan: You can have very relaxed talk – you know, on the social occasions, when you've had people to dinner and everybody had the right amount to drink, in which nobody is apparently trying to explore anything, but you may find something (Group: Mm.) quite exciting. (Peter: Mm, mm.)

Susan: Yes, because of course we mustn't devalue that sort of 'walkabout' talk, where one *is* trying to find out the sort of thing one might say (Peter: Oh yes.) that might please, and impress: there's nothing really wrong with using talk to impress other people, is there ? But one wouldn't want to do it . . . to have people who could only do that, and I think there are a lot of people like that.

Joan: I . . . I wasn't thinking of people at dinner parties trying to impress each other (Susan: No.), I mean there is a sort of just a pleasure in chatting away when you're all a tiny little bit high . . . (Peter: Mm.)

Peter: Letting it go where it will . . .

Joan: Yes.

Paul:	Do you find that at dinner parties or parties that . . . er . . . the kind of talk that satisfies you most is when you meet somebody and you discover something about their way of life which is foreign to you (Joan: Yes.), and that it therefore becomes in a sense, I mean, I find, it becomes, for me, almost subjecting that other person to a series of questions, and I love it when that person who answers expatiates, er . . . and then I can provoke with yet another question, because I'm interested in *that* little proposition which has been made.
Joan:	I don't think I'm as analytical as that. I mean, I'm always fascinated when you meet somebody whose had interesting experiences or has ideas (Paul: Mm.) which are new and will expatiate. I wasn't even thinking, you know, of meeting somebody now; I was thinking, you know, that sometimes if you can have a group of people that get on very well and they're very relaxed in a sort of holiday situation, they start to talk, almost idly, and . . . and something . . . er comes out of it, which is satisfactory to them – seems to be some sort of . . .
Susan:	I think that skill is available to quite a . . . er, you know, a very wide range of people, I mean, don't you, I mean, most people don't have dinner parties. (Joan: And I think children enjoy it.)

What talk is mostly used for?

	But, you know, it seems to me, just ordinary people. Isn't this sort of talk that (Group: Mm.) goes on among neighbours . . .
Joan:	And in pubs. (Susan: And in pubs.)
Peter:	Launderettes. Though I've never heard it.
Susan:	People just getting very interested in talking about – you know, sheets, and socks and things like that, I mean, I . . . I know I do.
Paul:	This sort of comparing notes with other people? (Susan: Yes.) Sharing your experiences?

Susan: You're not even doing that, because you *know*,
            you can *see* what colour their sheets are, you . . .
            it . . . you're mastering the relationships, even the
            transitory relationship with somebody else in the
            launderette . . . (Paul: Mm, you're . . .) (Group:
            Yes, mm.)

Paul: So if I want transitory relationships I must go to
            my launderette [*laughter*]. What fascinating doors
            you open. [*Laughter*.] [*Pause*.]

Susan: So I think that . . . that kind of talk although the
            content . . . er . . . may seem to be very down-to-
            earth, like sheets or whatever, er . . . may in fact
            not,

Talk as gesture – social solidarity.

            you know, obviously the content isn't important,
            but the social relationship is.

Joan: And that would . . . people could do that.

Susan: I think most people can.

Joan: That is a skill that . . . or whatever, that you would
            expect a good talker to have.

Susan: Er yes, or . . . or . . . but . . . and I think most
            talkers do, do have. Unless they really do have
            tremendous problems within their personality.

A new section:

Paul: Is it something which kids have in embryo and
            develop ? Do they . . .

Casting around:

Joan: I think before adolescence they naturally have it,
            don't they ? unless it's been inhibited. I mean, if
            you go into an infant or a nursery school they'll
            all come up and and, you know, about anything
            that comes into their heads. Quite easily.

Paul: And certainly if you see two kids absorbed in each

187

	other, playing, they seem to have no difficulty at all in sustaining dialogue.
Joan:	No.
Paul:	One wonders what, in fact, one did as a kid.

Reminiscences:

	How, you know, you go out after mid-day meal, you come back at teatime, and you were cycling round, or playing in the gutter and you were absolutely content with two or three other people. (Peter: Mm.)
Joan:	It's both sharing a world picture, and also making a new one between you, isn't it? (Paul: Mm.) Perhaps.
Paul:	Would it be true to say that the . . . er . . . single child erm . . . or the child who is ill-adapted for some reason or other . . . does have very real difficulty in making this sort of contact?
Joan:	They invent companions, don't they, quite often? Not (Paul: Yes, yes.) not, certainly just . . . (Peter: Mm.)
Paul:	I found in adolescence, you see (Peter: Sometimes they're right.), that I couldn't indulge in this kind of talk (Joan: Yes.), but I mean (Susan: No, er . . .) I could form a relationship with one other person without all that much difficulty, but the prospect of . . . of forming even the casual relationship of joining a group of people who were going to go for a walk . . . erm . . . in adolescence I found very very difficult indeed. It took many years, in fact, to learn how to indulge in sort of fragmented, gossipy, talk. (Peter: Mm.) And even now I think I still slightly prefer the kind of gossip which tries really to explore the situation. (Peter: Yes I know what you mean. I know what you mean.)
Peter:	Er . . . yes . . . a sort of inability to be . . . erm . . . frivolous or playful or er . . . just to let it go where it will. (Paul: Mm.) Er . . . you know just like your

	whisky works, the talk might come up . . . hit on anything. Unfocused sort of talk.
Susan:	You mean . . . you find that difficult ? Or . . .
Peter:	Yes. I mean I think I've had some . . . not as . . . to such, to such an extent as Paul described, but er . . . er . . . I've often found it difficult to er . . .

Difficulties with small talk.

| | participate in the group that I've been in at the time, in er . . . when they haven't been doing anything in particular. So long as they start doing something particular, like a task of some sort, or going somewhere, then it's all right. But just, sort of sitting around chewing the fat . . . or . . . bantering . . . (Susan: Mm. I don't . . .), that sort of thing . . . |
| Paul: | Yes. This is why I find dancing in a sense better as a social occupation than just sitting around drinking, because if you're dancing nobody expects you to talk |

When you don't have to talk.

	so you don't have to make any sort of effort to be casual.
Peter:	Well one of the things about drinking is that . . . (Paul: I was just going to get you a drink . . .) the thing about drink is you don't have to talk . . . I mean that's, that's the point of the drink I think, isn't it ? You're really there to drink.
Joan:	Oh, I'm not sure.

Exaggerating to prove a point:

| Peter: | Well, this is, well, in Yorkshire we'll sit there for a whole evening and not say a word . . . because you're there to drink, and anyone who talks is interrupting the drinking, really. You know, they drink very slowly. I think this is, . . . whereas . . . you know . . . whereas you couldn't |

189

just go with somebody and sit down at opposite sides of the table, and talk to them, if you've got a drink in front of you, it's different. Because that can ... you're both operating the er ... sort of pretence you're really there drinking. So it's like working with somebody on digging a trench or something: you don't have to talk. Talk is incidental to the activity. So you don't have to make a thing of it.

Paul: And would one conceivably as a Southerner, say something about those uncivilized Northerners?

Joan: [*laughing*] You know I ...

Paul: Joan, will you have ... erm ... there's whisky, there's gin and ... or vodka, with Dubonnet or Campari ...

Joan: I'd love a drop of whisky if I might with a little bit of water thank you very much.

Paul: Susan, there is a tomato juice (Susan: Oh thanks.), or orange squash.

Joan: There is a sort of talk where you're just doing what children do I think very much at seven and eight – you're just playing around with words, you know, and capping each other's stories or ... er ...

Susan: But it's very strange because those children are very con ... they have a level of consciousness which is ... er ... fascinated by words, but I remember a great jerk at, I don't know when it was, 14, 15, 16, right out of that world and into another level of consciousness which I've never lost, and which I suppose some people call the loss of innocence, where I was seeing myself outside myself all the time. (Paul, Peter: Mm, mm.)

Is loss of spontaneity the inevitable price of progress?

And I've often ... tried to get back into that child-like state. I'm not saying I was unconscious of my

	surroundings, and I wasn't ... I wasn't unself-critical; it was just that whenever I did things, I was doing it and that was the end of it. And now I see myself all the time as a phenomena ... non ... er ... and obviously something like that does influence your talk.
Joan:	I think this is the point of the drink. Er, you know ... if you've had ...
Susan:	Yes. Well, that's probably why I don't, you see, because I ...
Joan:	It just slightly removes your inhibitions.
Susan:	You think ... do you think it's inhibited, then, to see oneself as a phenomenon?
Joan:	It's inhibiting, yes.
Peter:	It's inhibiting of talk. Because I mean when ... if you're watching yourself all the time you're always saying, 'Well why should I do this rather than that?' Or, er, 'That laugh's a bit false, isn't it?' There was a period in my life when I couldn't laugh (Joan: Mm.), because I was always watching myself laugh and then I'd find ... I'd find myself being artificial ... you know, there's something false about it.

Do some situations *provoke* performances?

| Joan: | And when I was teaching and even ... no, not now so much, but when I was teaching, I occasionally sort of removed myself and could hear myself teaching, and that was terrible, you know, because you sound like Joyce Grenfell and all the rest rolled into one, or something of the kind, and you just can't go on. Particularly, you know, in a class where you're getting no feed-back much. (Peter: Mm.) |
| Susan: | But I wondered for a ... for a great mass of people that jolt actually never ... never comes? (Peter: Mm.) I mean it was very very earthshaking for |

me, and I've never been able to get back previous to it. But I wonder from the nature of most people's talk when I hear them . . . I was next to three people in a pub last night, three journalists talking about how they were going to take over the paper . . . I mean, they were all very very drunk. And their talk was just so riddled with badly thought out . . . you know rubbish, revolutionary rubbish and cliches, every other word was a swear word, yet they were all utterly absorbed the three of them in what each of them was saying, but they were saying, to me as an outside listener, and they . . . I could tell that they in fact never would take over the newspaper. In fact, they thought they would, the way they were talking. And I thought well . . . these people, perhaps you're right, they have progressed backwards through being able to drink . . . , and I think of it as a back . . . backward progress, [*laughing*], because I'm very prejudiced against being drunk [*laughing*]

Joan: I wasn't suggesting being drunk [*laughing*] . . .

Susan: But they had . . . they had lost that inhibition (Joan: Yes.) and in losing it they lost something which I thought (Joan: Mm, mm.) was very, very valuable. I mean, if they could have heard themselves . . . or maybe they'd never had it in the first place to prevent themselves talking such utter idle rubbish.

Joan: But they were using this to let off steam, rather than to form a plan of action or . . .

Susan: And maybe they were using it to try to like each other more (Joan: Yes.) and to cement each other (Joan: Mm.) in some . . .

Peter: Is this self-consciousness just a sort of necessary concomitant of rationality ? Erm, in other words, as soon as you . . . if you could get to the stage where you see everything as not necessarily the way it is, it didn't have to be that way (Susan:

Mm.), but it's just – you know, a sort of contingent, and it could have been otherwise, and er (Susan: Yes, yes.) especially when you see social behaviour and conventions and all the rest of it . . . (Susan: Yes.), you know, that's not god-given any more (Susan: Yes.), then you look at everything yourself in a different light. (Susan: Yes, yes.)

A balanced view of society might be necessary for self-awareness.

Erm, in other words, as soon as you see, erm, phenomena in terms of abstractions (Susan: Mm.) and sets of possibilities and so on, which is a very necessary stage of thinking (Susan: Mm.) I mean it's what liberated the Greeks, when they went to Asia Minor and saw people behaving differently (Susan: Mm.) and so on, so they say . . . erm, so that, you know, they became conscious that it's this, and not that (Susan: Mm.), rather than being unconscious, because they were only being aware of the one way (Susan: Yes, yes.), well, when this happens to you, it operates on yourself just as much as all the things you look at (Susan: Mm.), as all the phenomena outside . . .

Susan: And it must radically alter your social behaviour.

So it affects your talk.

Peter: . . . so you see yourself as a phenomenon . . .

Susan: Yes. You know, any amount of drink wouldn't stop me doing that, I don't think, now; any amount of sort of . . .

Peter: But perhaps that's an aspect of alienation, or something.

Joan: I think . . . I don't know, it sounds silly to say you've got to forgive yourself . . .

Paul: Peter, whisky, or gin and dubonnet, or gin and campari, or . . .

Peter: Er, whisky, I think, Paul.

Joan: But, you know, if you accept that you are a phenomenon, and an inadequate one, as we all are . . .

Susan: Oh I don't know [*laughing*]! Speak for yourself [*laughing*]!

Joan: Well, I think we . . .

Susan: Oh all right . . . I'm very arrogant you see [*laughing*].

Joan: Then I think you can be much more interested in all the other phenomena, because there's not very much you can do.

Susan: But you see, you know this kind of talk Paul (Joan: Yes.) was talking about, where one sort of sits back and sort of restrains oneself from saying that and says (Joan: Yes.), 'That's very interesting, could you develop that?'

An acquired skill.

            You can't . . . you couldn't possibly do that unless you saw yourself as . . . er, as a phenomenon in that situation – unless you could for the moment see that what was more important than anything was your role, and shutting up, and letting somebody else do it. (Joan: Well . . .) You need to feel less real, in that situation . . . in order to let other people . . .

Joan: I don't know why you can't just not feel it's your role, but really feel more interested in the activity of the other person talking, even though the talk, the quality of the talk (Susan: Yes. Paul: Mm.), looked at detachedly may not be so good. I mean it's . . . it's after all . . . like all teaching, isn't it? Er, you can all do most things better than the children you teach. But it's much more fascinating to . . . to have them do it – it's more rewarding, more interesting

It can become natural to you.

> . . . it's not a question of pretending, is it?

Susan: Oh, I don't know, I don't think it is pretence. But do you feel when erm when er . . . you're talking . . . it's so different in the teaching situation . . . but in the peer group situation, or in the peer group situation with kids when that can be arranged, are you still more interested, or doesn't it arise, by what you hear yourself say, or what you hear other people say?

Joan: I'm much more interested in what I hear other people say. I know what I'm going to say. (Group: Oh!)

Susan: Do you?

Joan: Well, no, not completely, but er . . . particularly with children, I think, I'm much more . . . and with students . . . interested in what they're going to say than what I'm going to say.

Susan: I sup . . . I . . . I get a great deal of surprise out of what . . . what I say, still.

Joan: Yes, I think . . . I think I do at times, I suddenly come out with something that was ind. . . . rather . . .

Peter: I mean that . . . obviously one of the elements in progress is, er, an extension of control of consciousness . . . er, and you said that one of the . . . the, er, features that you're most pleased about in your, your own mature talk is that you – you surprise yourself with it,

Delight in hearing yourself thinking a new thought.

> which suggests a sort of absence of control.

(Group: Mm.) I mean it's, it's . . . those things are unplanned, they just come. (Joan: And –) Is it – I mean, I just thought, you see, I . . . I was going to say before that, and that sort of rather takes the wind out of it, but, um, just as in all these courses where they teach decision-making and so on, the processes used to be aware of a problem, formulate their problems as problems, state the problem properly

How is this compatible with control and discrimination?

(Joan: Mm, mm.), you know, and then – then see that there are a number of alternative lines forward and so on, so, erm, maybe the, you know, the good talker is aware of, all the time, of taking up options, making decisions between alternatives of what he might say, and being conscious about the – you know – why he decides one way or the other – that, that sort of consciousness. But that would be – that's a very different sort of thing from this sort of existential 'fresh leaps'.

Paul: Don't you find, though, sometimes while ... while indulging this self-consciousness, nevertheless you find words in your mouth, ideas in your head, that you (Peter: Mm.) didn't know were there, in very much the same way, presumably, as when you write a poem. (Joan: Mm. Peter: Mm.) You have, in a sense, perhaps an overall plan, erm – with a specific direction that you're going in (Peter: Mm.), and then an image, or a phrase, comes into your head, quite without being commanded.

Peter: Now this is the elements of language that isn't a skill, isn't it? (Paul: Yes.) It can't be ... you know, described as a skill.

Paul: But it may be that ... I just don't know – I think this may be wrong but let's try it:

Trying out a new idea without a sense of risk:

it may be that, um, you have to develop to the point where you're relaxed enough to allow these ideas to bur. ... to burgeon?

Peter:	Perhaps the skill is, you know, getting yourself into the sort of situation where that can happen ?
Joan:	Yes. Well, we said earlier, didn't we . . . about not . . . about leaving things fluid and . . . (Group: Mm.) . . . you know, it's the Keatsian thing, really, though I'm sure that . . . really exciting speculative ideas and really exciting, um, artistic creations come from that sort of relaxed situation in which nobody is – is pre-empting anything that's going to happen. It . . .
Peter:	It's relaxed, and yet it's often a state of high excitement.
Joan:	Yes. You're in a state of high excitement because you're setting out on an adventure and you don't know where it's going to land you. (Paul: Mm.)

Leads to a satisfying mutual understanding:

	But you're prepared to do it – you're prepared to do it with other people in a talk situation.
Susan:	Everybody in a situation like that has to play the game, though. It only takes one person to . . . (Joan: Mm, absolutely right.) . . . play it off centre. I mean if one of us was trying to push a particular line, now, or if one of us was taking over the chair . . . er, that game would . . . er . . . be spoilt, wouldn't it ?
	[*Pause.*]
	Another thing I find you have to be willing to do in a situation like this is not to . . . hang on to every single bloody idea that comes into your head . . .

Talking involves waiting your turn, and maybe missing it.

I mean (Peter: Mm.) you have to be prepared to . . . let it go. Often . . . I noticed it while you were talking just now, I had something that I wanted to say, but I both had to listen to you and to hold on to (Paul, Peter: Mm.) what I wanted to say, then,

	had I then got the chance to speak, I would have *said* what I wanted to say and I would have craftily made it relevant to what you [*laughter*] had just said – and I realize ...
Peter:	That of course is the trick of writing (Susan, Joan: Yes.) that you don't have to lose all this.
Susan:	And really it's something I take for granted now which I know I found very painful about 10 years ago – you know. (Peter: Yes.) It makes one ... people like —, sit there silently. (Paul: Mm.)
Peter:	Yes. Mm. Now for a kid, I mean it must be incredibly difficult (Susan: Mm.) to abandon some ... a good idea, possibly forever.
Susan:	It's 'Sir! Sir!' ... you see it, don't you ? (Peter: Mm.)
Joan:	It's when ... they make their own, you know, chosen groups without teacher, they don't abandon then, do they ? It all comes out together.
Peter:	Yes. Ineffectually of course, because nobody hears it because ...
Joan:	But there's some sort of a consensus comes out together, too, isn't there ? I'm thinking of some of the transcripts.

Apparently undisciplined talk can result in group agreement.

| Paul: | Yes, because I think when you say something that's excited you, you don't merely want to voice it, you want it to be commended, certainly commented on, |

Most of us need encouragement.

| | but you're much more pleased ... if someone actually smiles and nods and says, 'Yes, that is so.' |
| Peter: | Mm, sort of to validate it really. |

So we encourage Paul:

| Joan: | Mm. |

198

Susan:	Mm.
Joan:	Mm.
Susan:	Yes, mm. [*Laughter.*]

So he goes on:

Paul:	Mm. This I think is the difficulty that some kids do experience, that they don't get that – a comment or a commendation.
Susan:	When they're just in a group of kids (Paul: Yes.) especially, this must be . . . is that, is that a skill though ? A talk skill ? That people should have, to be able to say the odd 'Mm' and, 'That's interesting' ? And then I think that through saying it, you do eventually begin to mean it, but I suppose some people . . .
Peter:	Do . . . yes. I'm sure it is. I mean it's one that I . . . I learnt from . . . interviewing kids on tape . . . which I've done a bit of in course of this, you know, present work. And . . . er, to make a good tape the secret is to get as little of yourself as possible.

Teachers particularly need to know how to make room for others to talk.

	(Susan: Mm.) You always find when you go back over the tape you said too much, and you distracted kids from what they were going on to. Er . . . so you, you know, you sort of train yourself, just to say, 'Mm', and only to intervene and give a prod, a question, only if it's absolutely necessary.
Susan:	Doesn't it take ages to train yourself ? (Peter: Gosh, yes.) Maybe you learnt better than I did.
Paul:	It's the same sort of training that one wants in the teacher. (Joan: Yes. Peter: Yes.) It's not simply the interview – tape situation.
Susan:	In that . . . when I got the group* in the 'TV Homeviewing' (sorry) . . . I . . . I gave specific

*of student-teachers in a College of Education.

instructions not to do this, not to interview question and answer. I wanted them to get kids to talk about programmes they'd liked, and what they handed in, their transcripts, they were *all* question and answer. (Paul, Peter: Mm.) One sentence question, the other sentence reply. It was really strange, even though I'd given them ever such explicit . . . (Paul: Mm.) . . . I tried to hand on to the students *my* experience, in other words (Peter: Mm.), and yet they had to go back to Stage A. (Peter: Mm.)

Paul: This might be very fascinating to have a small transcript of this sort of thing. (Joan: Yes. Peter: Mm.)

Susan: Oh yes. Well I have . . . I have got them of course.

Peter: This goes back to what er . . . you said, you know, the . . . that time before in the Institute, about, erm, when you'd been talking to a 7 year old kid, or something like that, and how bored you'd been [*laughing*], but you'd conscientiously talked to him.

Susan: Yes – do you remember that, Paul?

Peter: Using your skills!

Paul: Yes, well, I think, you see, I found it, . . . I was reflecting on what you said earlier this afternoon. I had a . . . a common-paper session, therefore with fairly experienced, third-year (Joan: Mm.) students, analysing a scene from *Macbeth*, in fact. And . . . er . . . for a lot of the time I was in one sense bored, because they were coming out with the ideas that I expected them to come out with, but I was of course not showing my boredom . . . I was commending them: 'Yes, that's sound. Any comments on that? Where would we put that in the total structure of our essay?' And then one of them came up with something that I'd never thought of. I had to get him to explain it to me first of all, because he does have some difficulty with language, but there did seem to me an insight that really did excite me.

Should the talk *skills*, as well as what is said, be the focus of the teacher's attention ? (Inevitably, the students focus on the *content*.)

        (Peter: Mm.) But then I had to be careful not to let, as it were, my excitement over that . . .

Susan: . . . to show too much approval because that . . .

Paul: . . . to show too much approval . . .

Susan: . . . because it isn't really fair, is it ?

Paul: No. And also, as it were, to upset the balance of the construct we were making – it was merely one element in the dramatic effect (Susan: Mm.) of verse, and I had to try and relate it, or get them to relate it, to what we'd previously said.
[*Pause.*]

Peter: I wonder whether . . . a group ever really makes a construct like that ? I mean, I wonder whether that's just er . . . er . . . whether we only imagine that, and, in fact, what the benefit of a thing like that is a whole of a . . . very disparate thing for the individual in the group ?

Do we all come away from a discussion with a different sense of what's gone on ?

Joan: I don't know. I . . . I taped the same group [College of Education students.] when . . . in the first year, with a colleague of mine, and then in the third year just before they went out . . . you know, discussing something (Peter: Mm.), and I felt they . . . and I played it back to them and we talked about it . . . and I felt this third year discussion . . .

Peter: . . . could document their progress ?

Joan: Yes. Well, I . . . I'm trying, sort of, hoping, to find something like this. Erm, I thought, by the end, that there was excitement, and the . . . the amazing thing was that there were *enormously* long pauses, while they waited, and let other people come in.

> And quite long utterances, and then very long pauses. And ... er, it seemed to me at the end there was a construct.

The shared construct a sign of progress ...

> I haven't looked at it closely enough – it's one of these tapes that's sitting there to be worked on at some time. And that they did all get something out of it.

Peter: They all got the construct? It wasn't just an abstract thing that was in the air in between them? You know, which you could get by looking at the total effect ...

Joan: I don't know. I don't know. I ma ... I got them to write something first. This is ... this is interesting because with the other group I got them to talk first and write after. With this lot I said well, write something first – so that they'd all had a personal approach. There was three – two poems, actually. Erm, and then they said they could never have got so much out of the discussion if they hadn't had this personal foray on it first ... but they did all seem to feel that they had got a lot out of it, and they certainly had advanced in whatever we're discussing: progress in talk – you know, they were ... they were ... I was there, I think I said two things, and nobody, really, was interested in what I [*laughter*] had to say, you know.

Paul: So they were more confident?

Joan: Much more confident.

Paul: And they were really taking charge (Joan: Mm.) of the discussion, and they'd also learnt the social (Joan: Yes.) acts of listening and participating fully.

Joan: Yes. And, I mean, this is not interesting except to me, but some of the people who did contribute an enormous amount had not previously ... (Paul: Yes.) ... found it easy to do so. (Paul: Yes.) And I did feel that they . . . they had made something between them. (Paul: Yes.)

They achieve creative group talk.

[*Pause.*]

Our own group exploration has led us to perceive one important aspect of progress. That's why we pause?

Paul: I found another aspect . . . talking in a social situation with someone like John, because every now and then he will recount an episode from his life,

We move to a totally different skill: the raconteur . . .

when, for instance he was living in Canada for a year, possibly working on a newspaper or working in a bar (Susan: Mm.), and he has held me and one or two other people absolutely silent while he's talked for about forty minutes (Susan: Yes, some people have that skill) recounting an episode. I couldn't do that. (Susan: No, I couldn't.) I wouldn't have the confidence to start (Susan: I couldn't dramatize . . .), or the dramatic skill (Susan: No.) to present it, and whether this is something that is purely individual – you know, some people can paint pictures, and others can't, and one leaves it at that,

Something we can't all be.

or whether it's something one wants to develop in other people . . .

Joan: Well, I would have thought it was individual, really.

Susan: There's nothing worse is there than a *bad* raconteur?

Joan: Oh no [*laughing*].

Susan: And I mean I'm conscious of not being very good at it, so I'll mumble and cut it pretty short (Paul:

| | Mm.), whereas, you know, somebody like John, you're laughing from the very first sentence, you're engaged because you . . . of the confidence in them to make you. They usually are funny (Paul: Yes.) stories, aren't they, that people recount. Well, they're . . . they're always very emotionally charged – they're either very tragic, or very funny. One . . . one suspects that the original situation wasn't so charged [*laughing*]. (Paul: Yes.) I . . . I can feel John censoring it as he goes along . . . |

Paul: Yes: 'I won't put that in – very uninteresting that bit was', yes. [*Laughs.*]

Susan: And that . . . that . . . that of course is the skill of the raconteur, I suppose.

Joan: It's a literary construct, isn't it, and I mean some people have greater skill in doing that than others I think. And it's not something you do . . . I don't know. Is it something you do as a group?

Susan: Well, that's the sort of skill that people try to get kids to develop, isn't it? (Joan: Mm.) To stand . . . to do this sort of . . . er . . . monologue . . . (Group: Mm.) of what happened, and . . . that sort of thing. (Paul: Yes.) I . . . well, I think perhaps it is one of those things you're just born with, or . . .

Paul: I think this ties up, you see, – this business about getting kids to do it, with my feelings about formal debate: that's another thing that we – at any rate we *used* to try to get kids to do. To make a lengthy statement.

Another kind of monologue – formal debate.

(Peter: Mm.), and I've always felt it wasn't right, that far more useful was . . . was this sort of discussion . . . because the other were . . . are . . . was a skill that was available in only a very abnormal or peculiar situation. How often are we required to do that?

Susan: It's strange because the people who thought up the debate form must have thought that somehow that was microcosmic of, I don't know, human behaviour, whereas I tend to think that this sort of talk, now, is microcosmic and essential:

We go back to what we see as the crucial process:

that through doing this one's learning about all sorts of more complex intervals, and a child who can master the holding of an abstract idea and the interest in reaching consensus, or the understanding that if you don't reach consensus, it's not the end of the world, and so on, seems to me better prepared in all sorts of areas of human relationships, if that doesn't sound too romantic. (Paul: Mm.)

Paul: No. I think I would agree. And you know, this sort of ties up . . . OK, we've been talking about what *is* progress, and I think one might also want to consider what *kind* of progress does one want to . . . er . . . precipitate, encourage, as a teacher?

Progress in talk central to all progress?

Joan: It is the ability, probably, as Susan said, to be able to look at yourself detachedly, and to entertain, or extend, courtesy to other people to be themselves. And this is not only . . . purely intellectual thing, is it?

We sense that we are reaching our finale:

Susan: No, and I think it's very important in ordinary day to day things like marriage. [*Laughter*.] You know, if you can actually hear yourself saying . . . you know – rationalizing, and saying something wasn't your fault, blaming the other – when you really know it's yours ... I mean, you can't get beyond the first few sentences without laughing at yourself – I mean it's impossible to actually have a very embittered argument once you've got the ... did you see that programme on couples who never talk to each other ? Some *Man Alive* programme. I think we must have talked about it at the time.

Joan: One of the really awful sanctions, isn't it, is 'I won't speak to you.' (Group: Mm.)

Paul: I remember saying to somebody once ...

Susan: Of course children use that, as well.

Paul: ... making a statement and getting a categorical 'No', and then I went on to say, 'What I ... why I brought the subject up is ... is because I want to *discuss* it. I don't want the subject ended by a categorical "no".' [*Laughter*.] 'I want an explanation of why you say no, why you feel, and I want you to listen to me to ... at any rate to understand my point of view. I'm not necessarily wanting to persuade you, but at any rate I want to make clear what I feel and why.' So that ... this *is* important – this ties up with ... with ordinary (Group: Mm.) discussion in the classroom. Courtesy, and an open intellectual mind ... erm, a realization that perhaps my formulation 'No', is not necessarily the end, that there might be alternative ways of looking.

Susan: And er that ... and that sort of self criticism extends to cutting short what you're going to say, in the realization that you might be very boring, being on the watchout for that people are glazing over – that the subject may become ... that you've over-contributed, all those sorts of things. (Paul: Mm.) And that – er – in your ... in that situation you've just mentioned that you might rabbit on. I remember discussing whether there was a god or not one night very late with ... 'and he didn't ... he didn't [*laughter*] really want to discuss it, and it was probably more important for me to realize that, than to go on and on and on, trying to get him to say whether he did or didn't, you know? All those sorts of skills – *not* talking something out (Paul: Mm.) which the other person really doesn't want to . . . not going on and on, which I think is what a lot of teachers tend to do. They seem to be immune to the bore . . . you know, to how boring they're being. [*Pause.*] I see the drink has made [*laughter*] *you* all glaze over! [*Laughter.*] I told you it was a myth!

2. Our Tentative Conclusions

1. We shouldn't over-value the ability to engage in talk – some of our best friends don't talk, very much; and we don't love them the less. Some people choose not to operate in this way; have other concerns, other skills.

   But we may regret such an inability in ourselves, and we may feel it can limit our pleasure in life. We may, as parents or teachers, wish to help a child who feels so limited.

2. There is such a thing as good social talk that is not in any sense intellectual, analytical, exploratory. It may be a means of building and cementing relationships. Children appear to have this skill from very early on; and it is one that some people appear rather to lose than develop, through growing inhibitions. (We should want to help children retain this skill even though we accept that all inhibitions are not necessarily harmful: they can enable us, we suggest, to participate more fruitfully in group discussion, and to restrain ourselves from being merely foolish.)

3. Progress in talk must be partly simply a question of growth – linguistic, intellectual, social, emotional. There is obviously a stage in a child's development before which he is just not interested in abstract ideas, or willing to pursue any topic in talk for any length of time.

4. Progress seems to involve the ability to talk on an increasingly wide range of topics, and in a wide range of social situations. We consider the skill of the raconteur and suggest that this is perhaps a very special creative skill that one accepts not everybody possesses, nor need possess.

5. Fundamentally we see progress as depending upon the development of what one might call humanity, and certain social qualities and skills – concern, generosity, courtesy, humility:

   – being sufficiently interested in someone else to ask them questions, and listen to their answers;
   – being prepared to let someone have his head; allowing him time and space to formulate and reformulate an idea without interrupting him; and to support him with little encouraging noises;
   – being prepared to hold one's own point, or interest, temporarily in abeyance so that one can help someone else in his formulation; and so that the main thread of the discourse is not lost;
   – being prepared even to lose the chance of voicing an idea because the other person, or the mainstream of the argument is more important;
   – being able to participate in the formulation of a group construct to which all have contributed and now subscribe.

6. And such qualities and skills can only develop with increasing self-confidence, when the participants feel relaxed and totally unthreatened:

   – I don't have to win this argument to prove myself;
   – I don't have to defend my present views against attack;
   – I am not engaging in a conflict at all but some sort of exploration in the company of like-minded people;
   – I can therefore concentrate on the intellectual exploration, not on the effect I am making; not on the social relationships at all.

   We suggest that progress involves being able to do this not merely with a small group of intimates but with increasing ease in a large gathering of comparative strangers.